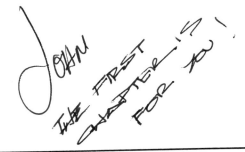

THE SECRETS OF
ACTION
SCREENWRITING

From "Popeye Points" to "Rugpulls"

by William C. Martell

Hammer Productions
Los Angeles, California

William C. Martell
HAMMER PRODUCTIONS
10915 Bluffside Dr.
Suite 104
Studio City, CA 91604
email - wcmartell @ compuserve.com

TABLE OF CONTENTS

INTRODUCTION

THE ACTION FILM has been with us since the beginning of cinema. In fact the first fiction film ever made, Edwin S. Porter's "The Great Train Robbery", was an action film. From the brutal gangster films of the thirties (like "Public Enemy" and "The Roaring Twenties") to the sophisticated private eye films of the forties ("The Big Sleep"), to the cynical and violent post World War 2 films of the fifties ("Rogue Cop", "The Line Up", and "House Of Bamboo"), the slick escapism of the sixties (the James Bond films), the seventies paranoia films ("The Parallax View" and "Three Days Of The Condor"), the glossy spectacle films of the eighties ("Die Hard" and "Lethal Weapon") to the nineties ("Face/Off" and "The Fugitive"); action films have always been in vogue. While horror films, musicals, and romances go through cycles of popularity; film audiences never tire of Action.

Action is also the foundation of many other genres. It was common in the forties and fifties to rework popular action scripts into Westerns ("The Last Of The Comanches" and "The Fiend Who Walked The West"). Science Fiction films like "Aliens" and "They Live" are basically action films with monsters instead of mobsters. Mysteries, Thrillers, Adventures, Suspense Films, and even some Comedies and Romances base their plots on conventions of the action film.

Everything you learn in this handbook can be adapted to whatever genre or sub-genre is popular at the moment. The car chase becomes a horse chase. The gun battle uses lasers. The suspense isn't built around our hero hiding a corpse from party guests, but our hero hiding the huge hole in his trousers from the party goers (an overused farce comedy device which still manages to get a laugh).

Because the Action Film has always been popular, it's a good place for the novice screenwriter to break into the business. I will take you step-by-step, from outlining to character motivation to polishing your script. Sharing my experience as a professional screenwriter with seventeen produced feature films, most in the action and thriller genres.

TOOLS, NOT RULES

The purpose of this book is to give you the tools necessary to write an action or thriller screenplay, not to tell you how to write. There are places in the book where I might say "On page 25, THIS happens"... Those are guidelines, not part of some by-the-numbers formula which must be adhered to. If the Plot Point happens on page 24 or 26 or 32 or doesn't happen at all, depends on the individual script you are writing.

Instead of rules or formula, think of this book as a recipe. Follow the recipe and you'll end up with lasagna for six. Some of you may want to add extra garlic. Some may want to omit the onions, or add celery, or substitute spinach for ground beef. The recipe gives you the guidelines, and you get to season to taste. But be forewarned: Change too much of the recipe and you'll end up with something that isn't lasagna!

Okay, let's pre-heat the over to 425' and put on our chef's hats... Ready for some action?

WHAT'S THE BIG IDEA?

Your action script is going to start with an idea, but not just any idea... you need one that *rocks.*

Most of you probably know what "High Concept" means, but for those of you who don't: High Concept is STORY as star. The central idea of the script is exciting, fascinating, intriguing, and different. High Concept films can usually be summed up in a single sentence or a single image.

A bomb on a city bus will go off if the bus travels under 55 mph... and rush hour has just begun! When terrorists take over Alcatraz, threatening San Francisco with chemical weapons, a commando team depends on the only convict who ever escaped the island to show them the way inside. When genetically engineered 'perfect soldiers' go on a rampage, the last human soldier comes out of retirement to stop them.

If you can't distill your story into thirty words or less with an exciting central idea, you have a hard sell. Once the film is made, the studio's advertizing department will have to come up with a 30 second TV spot and a catchy line on the poster. When your film sells to a cable channel, TV Guide will have to come up with a one sentence description. Foreign sales make up more than 60% of a film's earnings, so your story should have an idea clear enough to be understood regardless of language. If you can't see the poster, you've got a hard sell.

Here are some examples of High Concept:

An FBI agent uses high tech plastic surgery 'becoming' a terrorist leader in order to infiltrate his terrorist group and stop them from blowing up Los Angeles. ("Face/Off")

Anti-social cop tracks a serial killer who is knocking off people from a newspaper's list of World Class jerks... which includes the anti-social cop! ("The Dead Pool")

A housewife discovers that her meek computer-geek husband is actually an international spy like James Bond. ("True Lies")

Cowboys discover a lost valley filled with dinosaurs, and bring some back for a wild west show. ("Valley Of The Gwangi")

An L.A. Cop is partnered with an alien detective to track down an intergalactic serial killer who chameleons into his victim's form. ("The Hidden")

A man from the post-apocalyptic future is sent back in time to save the earth, but gets thrown into a mental institution when he tells someone his mission. ("12 Monkeys")

These are all big ideas, weird ideas. The poster for "Valley Of The Gwangi" shows cowboys on horseback herding and roping a T-Rex. When you see the poster, you almost do a double take. Cowboys? Dinosaurs? In the same movie? You want to know more. You want to see the film. That's High Concept.

Take a look at YOUR script. Is the IDEA behind it exciting and different? If you tell the idea to your friends, do they want to know more? Do they want to read your script? The idea behind your script will create the film's identity, so it must be memorable. It must have pizzazz. Your story can't just be cops track a serial killer, there are a million movies like that. Your script has to be something special.

Even with Brad Pitt and Morgan Freeman, two hot actors, "Seven" was sold with ads which described the 7 deadly sins. The sins were the concept which sold that script. We have forgotten the sins, and most of us are guilty of at least one of them. Even our two detectives were guilty of a couple of sins.

Here's a high concept serial killer idea: A town plagued by serial killings hires a renown tracker of serial killers as Sheriff. But soon, the townspeople realize their new Sheriff is a serial killer... of serial killers, and hopes to someday be KING of the serial killers.

Another idea: A serial killer picks up where Jack The Ripper left off, and begins killing prostitutes. Is he Jack The Ripper reincarnated? A pretty rookie cop is sent undercover as a prostitute to try and catch him. But that puts her life in danger. And how far will she go to catch the killer?

Your idea HAS to be different than the rest. It has to be unique. Have its own identity. Not just cops chasing a serial killer, but MORE. Both the killer and the cops must be different, and the venue must be unusual.

Someone once said that there are only seven basic stories which can be told. This means your big idea isn't likely to be something that we've never heard of before, but an interesting and unique variation on some story we have heard.

Cornell Woolrich has a novel called "Black Curtain" (filmed as "Street Of Chance") about an amnesia victim trying to uncover his past, who uncovers the frightening fact that he is a murderer.

In the 1970's, novelist David Ely came up with a Cold War variation. The mild mannered amnesia victim was brain washed to forget that he used to be a government assassin. Now as he tries to uncover his past, the CIA is out to kill him.

"Total Recall" makes it science fiction. The amnesia/brain wash victim goes to Mars to uncover his past, and finds out he was an interplanetary spy (and his own worst enemy).

Shane Black takes it back to earth in "The Long Kiss Goodnight", but makes the amnesia victim a June Cleaver like mom and housewife, who has to protect her daughter when she uncovers her past as a government assassin.

All are variations on the same idea, but given a new and exciting twist.

I've written two scripts for Martial Arts Star Don "The Dragon" Wilson. Don is the World Kickboxing Champ, so the script always has to showcase his talented feet... In a high concept action story.

In my HBO World Premiere movie "Grid Runners" ("Virtual Combat"), Don is a cop sent to track down the villain from a virtual reality fighting game used to train police, who has been cloned into reality... Only Don has never won against him in the game.

In "Night Hunter" Don is the last of the vampire hunters, trying to kill a family of vampires before the total eclipse allows them to multiply and take over Los Angeles. Neither idea sounds like a typical kick boxing movie.

In my HBO World Premiere movie "Crash Dive!", terrorists take over a US nuclear submarine and aim the missiles at Washington, DC... The only man who can stop them: A bookworm in the Navy's Engineering Division who knows everything about the sub.

Your idea has to be different. Growing up with James Bond and Nichols & May, I came up with a great script idea: "That's my son, the spy." Even James Bond has a mom, right? Well, this idea became garbage as soon as they made "Stop Or My Mom Will Shoot". The ideas are too similar.

There can't be ANY film out there with the same idea. If your script is cops & robbers, there better be something unusual about the characters, the venue, and the plot which makes it exciting and unique.

I have a script called "Wheels" about a pair of Viet Nam Vets who team up to solve a buddy's murder. All of the other members of their platoon are being killed one by one. Have you heard this one before? The difference: My two action leads are disabled. One is a paraplegic confined to a wheel chair and the other has suffered severe head trauma and is partially brain damaged. Brains and Brawn. Together, they're an action character; separately, they're in trouble. They need each other to survive. Your script must have a strong central idea which is the focus of the story, and different than any other film which has been made. That is High Concept.

ONE IS NOT ENOUGH

But one idea does not a script make. Your script should be FILLED with fresh, new ideas. In "Die Hard 3" we have a terrorist blowing up New York City... But that's just the beginning. The real plot is to rob the Fed Reserve Bank. PLUS we have the Simon/McClane revenge plot. PLUS the reluctant Sam Jackson character. PLUS the ticking clocks all the way through the film. PLUS the tunnel escape idea. PLUS the 'Simon Says' game. PLUS...

One idea isn't enough. You've got to have a dozen neat little ideas PLUS good writing PLUS an idea which is something we have never heard of before and EXTREMELY high concept (Cop Partnered With Dinosaur, The Magnificent Seven In Outer Space, Aliens On Earth). That's what will make your script attractive to producers. An idea they've never heard of and a script which keeps surprising them.

Even with all of these neat little ideas, remember the focus of the script is the Big Idea, the high concept. You don't want to confuse your audience with a bunch of ideas. Make sure your dozen fresh small ideas are somehow related to the Big Idea.

"Die Hard With A Vengeance" is a good example of small ideas revolving around the high concept of "Die Hard In New York". The mad bomber is using the explosions to cover up his robbery of the Federal Reserve Bank. He calls the police and plays "Simon Says" to give them clues to the bombs. Once on sight, deactivating the bombs requires solving a puzzle. The policeman being called is the man who killed the mad bomber's brother. Each small idea supports the concept and is part of the big idea.

Instead of distracting from the Big Idea, the small ideas focus on it and heighten it.

Use as many small fresh ideas as you can, to make your script constantly different and exciting. One good idea is a great start, but you've got to keep them coming. Don't worry about running out of ideas, and don't save a great idea "for the sequel". If the first script doesn't get sold and made, there is no sequel!

Having a high concept is no guarantee that your script will be any good (that's why the book doesn't end with this chapter), but it will help your script sell, and help it weave its way through the mine-field of development and production.

To show you the power of a good high concept, look at "Hard Rain"... a terrible script with a great high concept (an armored car robbery during a torrential flood using Jet Skis and speedboats). This script was sold, cast, made, and released on the basis of it's concept alone! Imagine how salable a GOOD script with an interesting high concept would be!

That is your mission, should you decide to accept it.

TIMELINE EXAMPLE

▽ UNREASONABLE FORCE ▽

5 — RESTAURANT: 3 MASKED MEN PULL VIOLENT ROBBERY! MURDER MRS. MENDOLSON!

(10) — PIER: INTRO HARRY (THE COKE DEAL) SHOOTOUT! PIER CHASE! HARRY'S PARTNER SHOT!

15 — HARRY'S NEW PARTNER: KELLY (SHE'S A GIRL!) THEY HATE EACH OTHER! Q+A RESTAURANT WITNESSES

(20) — TWIST ROBBERY WAS MURDER OF MRS. MENDOLSON!

25 — INTRO: WOODBRIDGE (VILLAIN), WILDER, ZUCKER (HEACH) + PLAN: SMUGGLING GUNS.

(30) — CLUE TO PEDRO. PEDRO'S APT: BIG SHOOTOUT! HARRY KILLS PEDRO.

[END ACT ONE]

35 — THE DEADEND. HARRY/KELLY: RELUCTANT BONDING (FORCED TO COOPERATE) "COWBOY" IS ONE OF ROBBERS.

(40) — CLUE TO BAR BAR (IT'S TOPLESS): VIOLENCE ERUPTS! SHOOTOUT... COWBOY KILLED.

45 — HARRY + KELLY AT PAWN SHOP: "THE BUTCHER" COMPUTER: LEAD TO ZUCKER ("THE BUTCHER")

(50) — BUTCHER SHOP: ZUCKER ALMOST KILLED BY SNIPER HINTS HE DONE IT.... CONFESSES... SNIPER! SNIPER ATTACK! ESCAPES.

55 ★ — A DAY AT THE PARK: HARRY KELLY (DISCUSS THE CASE) "HILL KLIEGS"?

(60) — HILL KLIEGS = PHONE # MENDOLSON'S PHONE NUMBER... MEET WITH MENDOLSON PARKING GARAGE SHOOT OUT MENDOLSON KILLED!

65 — CAR CHASE: HARRY KELLY CHASE MENDOLSON'S KILLER (WILDER)

(70) — ALLEY AMBUSH! HARRY KELLY SURROUNDED! KELLY IS KILLED!

[END ACT TWO]

75 — HARRY CALLED ON THE CARPET: IS HE RESPONSIBLE? DARK TIMES HARRY SUSPENDED.

(80) — TWIST KELLY IS ALIVE! WOODBRIDGE'S PRISONER HARRY GETS HIS GUNS!

(85) — WAREHOUSE HARRY ATTACKS! RESCUES KELLY! THEY TEAM UP! BIG SHOOTOUT!

(90) — HARRY vs. KELLY 15 BADGUYS: HARRY + GIANT / KELLY + WILDER: FORKLIFT JUST!

(95) — WOODBRIDGE ESCAPES BY BOAT BIG BOAT CHASE! SHOOT OUT ON THE WATER.

(100) — VERY PISTOL: GUN BARGE ≷EXPLODES≷ KELLY FIGHTS WOODBRIDGE! END!

[END]

TIMELINING

Action film producer Joel Silver says: "You've got to have a 'whammo' every ten minutes; an explosion, a car chase, a fight scene, to keep the audience interested." Silver believes this is the most important thing in action film, and he's probably right. Silver has made the most successful action films ever, and launched Schwarzenegger as an Action Lead in the low budget hit "Commando".

Pacing and Timing are critical to action films.

Long dead spots and an abundance of talk scenes will sink your script before it ever gets made. Action scripts contain action scenes and you've got to keep those car chases and shoot outs coming, or the audience will get up and leave.

Our job as action writers is to rupture bladders.

Your script should be paced so that there is NO time for the audience to get up and go to the rest room. They've spent $3 on a king sized Coca-Cola which is empty about halfway through the film. Now they're looking for that dead spot so that they can run to the bathroom. Your job is to make sure there are NO dead spots. So the timing on your script is critical. But how can you tell if you've got a 'whammo' every ten minutes before you've finished your script? Through "Timelining".

Some people use 3x5 cards to outline their scripts. This method doesn't work well with action scripts, because you have no idea how many minutes/pages each card represents. In action scripts, the duration of the scene is as important as the content. So I use a TIME LINE or a WHAMMO PAGE. This is similar to a 'beat sheet', which lists critical scenes, except it's broken down into five minute increments.

Start with a standard piece of eight and a half by eleven lined paper. On the top of the page, write the title of your script. You can just write "Title:" for now. Neatly number by fives, each line on the left hand side. Start with 5, end with 110. But between 30 and 35 skip a line, and do the same between 80 and 85. In those spaces, write "end Act 1" and "end Act 2" and draw a little box around them. Now CIRCLE numbers 10, 20, 30, 40, 50, 60, 70, 80, 90, 95, 100, and 105. Those are your 'whammos'. Put a little star next to 55. That's your midpoint, and will probably be an emotional turning point for your lead character. There.

Now you can look at the TIMING of your script without turning pages or trying to figure out how much time a 3x5 symbolizes. You know that each line is 5 minutes of screen time and 5 pages of script. You know that every ten minutes something exciting is going to happen until Act 3, when your script becomes wall-to-wall action. You know that this film will mean at least one messy bladder explosion in every theater.
Now all you have to do is fill in the blanks...

Grab a note pad and write "menu" at the top. Now number the lines from one to five on the left hand side and start brain storming scene ideas for your script. When you get five of them, keep numbering as you go. Write down character scenes, emotional scenes, plot scenes, romance scenes, and action scenes. Don't censor yourself. If you come up with an idea, write it down. If you get 27 ideas, flip to a new page and come up with some more. If you get 25 ideas, number the next line 26... You'd be surprised how that blank line will jog another idea from your mind.

Don't begin numbering up to 27, because then you'll choke up. How can anyone come up with 27 ideas? It's impossible. But anyone can come up with one idea at a time... and they add up.

Remember that you'll need at least a dozen action scenes. Try to come up with more, so you can choose the best. Here's where you try to come up with those "action scenes you'd like to see". A ROOFTOP car chase? Write it down! A fist fight in an elevator? Write it down! A shootout in a crowded bus station? Write it down! A western HORSE chase? Write it down! You'll need BIG action scenes and LITTLE action scenes. That way you can "build" your script to bigger and bigger climaxes.

And don't forget your climax. That HUGE topper action sequence that ends your script. Write it down! The more ideas you have, the more you can choose from. You should always end up with a numbered empty line at the end of your menu.

Once you have your MENU of ideas, it's time to pare them down into the best scenes. Try to find the theme or nexus which ties your action scenes to your plot and character scenes. You may come up with a kick-ass motorcycle chase, but it might not fit in with the rest of the story. So it's OUTTA THERE.

Once you have your best ideas, it's time to decide where to put them on your time line. It's best to start with your plot scenes, then add the character and emotion scenes, and save the action scenes for last. This way, the action serves your plot and character, not the other way around.

Not all scenes will last a full five pages, so it's okay to have more than once scene per line. In fact, most films will have about 45 scenes (give or take). That's about two scenes per line. But remember, BIG ACTION SCENES will take more pages than small ones. The car chase scene in "Bullitt" is TEN minutes long! One five minute segment where the hit men chase Bullitt through San Francisco's hilly streets. Then Bullitt turns the tables on them, and chases the hit men for five minutes on country roads... Until the hit men run into a gas station. BLAAMM! The ten minute car chase ends with a bang.

When you fill in your action scenes, remember that variety is the spice of life. Don't put two car chases or two shootouts right next to each other. In fact, car chases probably need to be separated by at least 30 minutes, unless you're doing a sequel to Walter Hill's "The Driver" or some other driving-based script. The point is to avoid being repetitious. One exciting shoot out after another can get boring! The key to a great action script is a balanced diet. Some fight scenes, some car chases, some shoot outs, some adventure oriented scenes (mountain climbing? Big stunts?)... A little of everything and not too much of one thing all at once.

Also, try to BUILD the action scenes from small to large. Remember, if you start with the end of the world, you have no place to go. So start small. I like to start with fist fights, move to small shoot outs, then the car chase, and end with a huge shoot out (like most James

Bond films). Sure, in between the car chase and the shoot out, there may be another fist fight... but this one pits our hero against five guys.

The action needs to escalate. Each action scene should be BIGGER than the one before it.

Have you seen "To Live And Die In L.A."? It has this killer car chase in the middle of the film... which is followed by a bunch of smaller action scenes which seem more suited to Act 1 than Act 3. Be careful not to use an "Act 1 Action Scene" in Act 3, or an "Act 3 Action Scene" in Act 1. Always save the best for last. You don't want the audience to be disappointed by the next action scene, and the best way to do that is to make each action scene BETTER than the last.

Another important element to consider in your timeline is how the action scenes relate to your lead character. The action in Act 3 will be MORE PERSONAL than the action in Act 1. Watch "Lethal Weapon" as an example. In Act 1, the action scenes have nothing to do with Danny Glover's character... But in Act 2 the bad guys start shooting at PEOPLE HE KNOWS, and by Act 3, they've kidnaped his daughter. Each action scene should draw the lead character DEEPER into the action, ending with the lead character's life on the line.

THE BEST ACT 3s use what I call "out of the fry pan into the fire" action scenes. A car chase ends in a crash, and the hero must run on foot, until he hits a dead end alley, where he gets involved in a shootout, then he climbs the fire stairs of a building, and gets involved in a rooftop chase. One action scene after another, with little down time in between. By Act 3, you've got the audience in the palm of your hand... and it's time to squeeze! Keep that action coming!

Timelines are also a valuable tool in studying existing action films. It's important to take apart films and see how and why they work, in order to learn how to improve your scripts.

So I suggest timelining some existing films to use as 'models'. Use a stop watch, a wrist watch, or put a clock with a second hand on top of your VCR. Now do a 'beat sheet' listing all of the plot, character, and action beats in a film... but also list the time when these events occur. I usually write when a scene ends: Car chase on street/23 (minutes into the film). Now adapt your beat sheet onto a time line, by placing everything within 5 minute increments.

One of the things you'll probably notice is a phenomenon I call "Chapterizing". Strangely enough, things will actually happen within five minute blocks.

For instance, in Richard Price's "Sea Of Love", 35 minutes into the film Al Pacino and John Goodman begin setting up dates with potential suspects. During the five minute segment from 35-40 minutes, they set up the dates, go to the restaurant and meet date #1, date #2, and date #3. Exactly 40 minutes into the film, Pacino meets date #4... Ellen Barkin. So that five minute "chapter" of "Sea Of Love" covers setting up the dates and meeting 3 suspects who we KNOW are not the killer.

The next five minute "chapter" gives us 2 minutes of Al and Ellen, and 3 minutes of tracking a grocery delivery boy who becomes a prime suspect. Exactly 45 minutes into the film, Al bumps into Ellen by accident, and they decide to go on a date. That 5 minute block concerns the things leading up to the date, and the date itself. 50 minutes into the film, the date 'ends' with Al and Ellen making love.

I don't know why films tend to "chapter out" into 5 minute segments like this. Maybe that's the way they were outlined, maybe that's the way they were edited. But it's a weird phenomena you can use to your advantage, by trying to find the "chapter title" of each five minute block. "Al and Ellen go on a date". "Al tries to propose marriage and blows it".

This will help you focus on what is the central idea of each sequence of events. Instead of aimless scenes which don't seem to build anywhere, we know from the time they set up the dates that they will find a suspect.

Each event in the five minute segment takes them CLOSER and CLOSER to finding that suspect. The segment ends when they've found her.

I suggest making timeline models of your favorite action films, to give you an example of how they're paced. You may find certain patterns in these timelines. For instance, there tends to be only two timelines for buddy cop films. "Red Heat" and "48 Hours" are almost identical when broken down this way.

After you've done several timelines, you might want to do an ABSTRACT model. Take similar films' timelines and look for patterns (like "Red Heat" and "48 Hours"). Then make a generic timeline which covers all of the films. This is a useful tool when you can't figure out what should happen next on YOUR timeline. But it can also work against you, by creating "cookie cutter" scripts where the most predictable thing happens next.

That's why I often use my abstracts to show me what NOT to do... By taking the formula and altering it, you can create twists and turns that audiences haven't ever seen before.

By timelining existing films, you will get a feel for what makes them work. Once pacing becomes part of your subconscious, you can throw away your timelines and abstracts and write from your heart.

Think of timelines as bicycle training wheels: for a while you need them just to keep balance, but soon you've learned to balance on your own and no longer need them. After a while, you'll be able to say "This needs a whammo", and write in the scene. Until then, using a timeline is a valuable tool in keeping the pacing of your action scripts tight...

And exploding a few bladders while you're at it.

THE VILLAIN'S PLAN

The most important element of an action film isn't the hero, isn't the sidekick, isn't the dialogue, and isn't the plot. The most important element of an action films is THE VILLAIN'S PLAN. Why?

Hitchcock said, "The better the villain, the better the picture". The Villain's Plan is the fuel for the plot. The Villain is going to do some dastardly deed, and the Hero must stop him. That means the hero is in a REACTIVE role, and the villain is in the ACTIVE role. When writing your action script, remember that the villain is your most important character.

Let's use "Die Hard" as an example. The Hero's desire and need is to reunite with his wife and children for Christmas. Is that an action movie? If you throw in a couple of fist fights and a car chase is it an action movie?
No.

But the VILLAIN'S PLAN in "Die Hard" is to rob the Nakatomi Corporation's safe of millions of dollars on Christmas Eve. That's an action plot. There is an exciting story even without John McClane.

In fact, if you were to delete all of the Bruce Willis scenes, you'd have an action film about Robbers vs. FBI agents. Maybe Agent Johnson ("no, the other one") would have been the hero. If Robert Davi's scenes were deleted, maybe Officer Powell would be the hero. But even without Reggie Vel Johnson, there would STILL be an action movie.

Because the Villain would still have a plan.

THE VILLAIN IS ACTIVE, THE HERO IS REACTIVE.

That's the second most important thing you'll learn in this book. You can have the most vile, un-lovable, ugly hero in the world, and as long as the Villain's Plan is good, we will still identify with the hero and root for him to save the day. Because the Villain's Plan is the fuel for action, not the hero's appeal. If you don't believe me, check out Lee Marvin in "Point Blank" or Mel Gibson in the remake version "Payback". In any other film these guys would be villains !

THE BIGGER THE VILLAIN'S PLAN, THE BIGGER THE MOVIE.

If your script is about a villain robbing the First National Bank in Omaha, it's a small movie. If the villain's plan is to rob every bank in Omaha on the same day, that's a medium sized movie. If your villain's plan is to rob Fort Knox, that's "Goldfinger". This is the third most important thing you'll learn in this book:

GIVE THE VILLAIN A BIG PLAN.

Don't just have the villain want to kill one person,

have him want to wipe out an entire TOWN.

The higher the stakes, the more we want our hero to STOP THE VILLAIN. Remember, the villain is the active character, so his plan has to be ACTIVE. He must want to DO something. Rob a bank, blow up a plane, assassinate the President, take over Chicago, steal government secrets from a high security vault, make a million dollar drug deal, go back in time and kill the mother of his enemy, take over a corporation, or create an earthquake which turns Nevada into beachfront property.

If the villain just wants to be left alone, you've got a dull film on your hands. Why? Because THE HERO is the character who just wants to be left alone.
Look at "Shane" or "The Gunfighter" or "Witness". The hero is trying to get through life without shooting anyone, then the Villain sets his plan into motion, and the hero must do something to stop him.

There's an Orson Welles film called "The Stranger" about a Nazi War Criminal hiding out in small town USA. He just wants to be left alone. Then an FBI agent comes to town and starts poking around. Who's the hero? Who's the villain?

Strangely enough, we begin to identify with the Nazi War Criminal because he just wants to be left alone. The FBI Agent has the active role, and in a strange way, he becomes the villain. We start to wish the FBI guy would just quit hounding this nice family man. Strange, huh? The result is an interesting, complex, film.
But NOT an action film.

So beware! If the villain's plan isn't ACTIVE and

AGGRESSIVE enough, he could turn out to be the one the audience identifies with! Then you're in REAL trouble.

MOTIVATIONALLY SPEAKING

The bigger the villain's plan the bigger the movie, so try to come up with some massive dastardly deed for the villain but make sure it's plausible, too. Remember, the Villain's Plan is the fuel for your film; if you use bad fuel, you aren't going anywhere. If the audience can't believe the villain can get away with it, or can't figure out why the villain would want to do it in the first place, they'll reject your film.

The Villain's Plan has to be the exact thing we'd do if WE were the villain. The villain has to be well motivated, even if he's a serial killer. He can't just kill nurses because he likes it, we need to know WHY. And the reason has to be a good one.

When someone asks why your villain did that, "Because he's crazy" isn't a good enough answer. We have to not only know WHY he's crazy (and it has to make sense and be psychologically sound) but his actions have to be logically tied into that insanity.

Watch "Manhunter" or "Silence Of The Lambs" (better yet, read the books by Thomas Harris) for an idea of how police use psychological profiles to nab serial killers. If you want to write a script with an insane villain, be prepared to do some research. You might start by reading "Mindhunter: Inside The FBI's Elite Serial Crime Unit" by John Douglas and Mark Olshaker.

TODAY'S PHYSICS LESSON

For every action there has to be a logical reason. Remember, every villain would be a hero if the story were told from his point of view. And any hero who does something for foolish or unexplained reasons is unbelievable. Same thing goes for your villain !

Everything is "Cause And Effect". Write that down and underline it. There is no such thing as coincidence. Everything happens as the result of cause and effect. Something happens which triggers something else, which triggers something else. For every action there is a reason, and it is your job as a screenwriter to know that reason.

FOR EVERY ACTION THERE IS AN EQUAL AND OPPOSITE REACTION

That means that if the villain jay walks, the cop doesn't draw his gun and shoot him. If the villain's plan is to kill everyone in our hero's family, the reason can't be that the hero once splashed mud on the villain's clothes... unless you're writing a satire like "Slaughterhouse 5". It's okay for actions to escalate (in fact it's required), but don't try skipping from loud words to machine guns. Punishments should always fit the crime, even if it's the Villain dishing out the punishment.

THAT'S INCREDIBLE!

The Villain's Plan shouldn't be so difficult and complicated that it becomes incredible. Every once in a while

I see a film where the Villain's Plan is so complex that there has to be an easier way for the bad guy to make a buck. A good example is Steven DeSouza's "Ricochet". It's a plot we've seen a hundred times before: Crook gets out of prison and decides to make hell for the guy who put him there. But in "Ricochet", John Lithgow goes to so much trouble to screw up Denzel Washington's life, you wonder why he doesn't just shoot the guy. Wouldn't it be easier? Quicker? Less chance of getting caught?

The same thing happens <u>again</u> to Denzel in Nick Kazan's "Fallen", but with a high concept twist. Once again he plays a cop, but this time the Crook isn't getting out of prison... He's going to the gas chamber. Before the Villain dies, he vows vengeance against Denzel. After the execution the Villain's evil spirit possesses the bodies of several people and goes on a killing spree... just to frame Denzel for the murders! I don't know about you, but if I were immortal, I'd <u>start</u> by killing Denzel, then find something fun and relaxing to do for the rest of time. Why not just kill him and get it over with?

Both villains are supposed to be a master criminals, but about halfway through these films the revenge plots becomes so silly and complicated that they look stupid. The minute the Villain's Plan begins looking silly, you're in big trouble. If the Villain's Plan doesn't work, neither will the movie!

The same plot was done better in J. Lee Thompson's "Cape Fear" (1962) where Robert Mitchum's plan is simply to follow and hound Gregory Peck until the man cracks. Mitchum's plan is so simple, that it's LEGAL (except for killing the family dog, which is probably a misdemeanor), and we worry that he'll actually get away with it. If you haven't seen the original version of this film, go out and rent it tonight.

Another lapse in logic occurs in this frequently written scenario: The villain has committed the perfect murder in order to take over a multi million dollar corporation from his partner. The cop starts nosing around, and discovers some minor evidence; not enough to convict, but enough to convince him that the villain is a murderer. In Act 3 the cop confronts the villain, usually at a dinner party or a country club.

What does the villain do? He pulls out a machine gun and tries to kill the cop. Why? So that the cop won't continue his investigation.

Wait a minute! If the cop didn't have criminal evidence before, he sure does after the villain shoots up a dinner party.

In "real life" the villain would probably just call his attorney, and fight it out in court... where he has a good chance of winning. If the villain absolutely HAD TO kill the cop, he would use another perfect murder scenario. Maybe siphon off the brake and steering fluids from the cop's car, then arrange a meeting late one night at the end of a long, winding cliff side road. It's important to question every single move your villain makes, and make sure it's logical and not incredible.

GEOMETRY LESSON

The shortest distance between two points is a direct line. In the old "Batman" TV show, every Tuesday night's episode would end with the villain getting ready to kill Batman and Robin. Did he pull out a gun and shoot them? No. The villains would always come up with some weird, complicated, Rube Goldberg device which would lower the Dynamic Duo into a vat of acid slowly... Giving them enough time in the first few min utes of Thursday's show to escape.

Why not just shoot them and get it over with? Were these villains stupid, or what? They NEVER won.

And not one of my friends in the third grade ever believed Batman and Robin might actually die. Usually by Thursday, we'd already figured out how they would escape the vat of acid.

Saturday Night Live once did a skit on this subject titled "Kill James Bond!" If you capture Bond, just kill him! Don't tell him your plan first. Just kill him! Good advice to the wanna-be Villain.

The villain's plan should be threatening to others.

It's nice to have the hero save himself, but if he can save the rest of the city, too, even better. In John Lange (aka Michael Crichton)'s "Pursuit", E.G. Marshall plays a political extremist who has set a canister of nerve gas to go off during the Democratic National Convention. What follows is a dangerous game of cat and mouse between the extremist and an FBI agent assigned to investigate him.

Not only is the FBI agent in danger, but if he doesn't outwit the extremist and find the canisters in time, millions will die. The Villain's Plan poses a major threat to others.

In "Cape Fear", Max Cady's plan poses a threat not only to Gregory Peck, but to his entire family, and anyone who helps him. Like the Private Eye he hires to protect his family (played by Telly Savalas).

Without a logical, well motivated, threatening villain's plan, you don't have a plot. And without a plot, what's the hero going to do?

Collect unemployment?

THE HERO'S JOB

The hero's job is to stop the villain. I know that sounds simple, but many action scripts seem to lose track of that somewhere along the line. Even in "Lethal Weapon", Riggs gets lost for a couple of scenes trying to talk down a suicide jumper. What was the villain doing while this was going on?

Sure, the Hero's character development is important, but whenever possible, try to let the characterization grow from the conflict within the plot. Don't paste anything on that doesn't move the plot forward. In a few chapters, we'll cover the hero's inner conflict; and I'll give you a few professional tricks on how to incorporate characterization into the plot. For now, let's just concentrate on his job... Stopping the villain

Since the Villain's Plan fuels the story, the hero has to be someone who gets in the way of the plan. "The fly in the ointment, the monkey in the wrench," as John McClane says in "Die Hard".

The hero can be a cop, a fireman, a private eye, a reporter, a regular guy, a pro-golfer, a lawyer, a scientist, a psychic, a sumo wrestler, or a weatherman. But whatever his day job is, it has to fit in with the Villain's Plan. If the villain is smuggling weapons into the country, the odds of a TV weatherman being the only one who can stop him are pretty slim. More likely, the hero of this story is going to be in the Coast Guard, or a Customs Agent, or maybe even a longshoreman working at the docks who sees something suspicious.

The hero's "day job" is a facet of the Villain's Plan. This is why there are so many cop heroes in films. Cops will naturally get in the way of any criminal activity.

It's called a "franchise" in the TV world.

A franchise is what places a hero in the line of fire week after week. You can have a cop show or a private eye show or a lawyer show, and you know criminal activities will be part of the story every week. But when you make your lead a matronly mystery writer (like on TVs "Murder She Wrote") you have to keep coming up with weird reasons why she's involved in solving crimes. After a while, you wonder why people keep moving to Cabot's Cove... that town must have the highest murder rate in the nation!

My advice on hero's day jobs is to be creative. Don't make her a cop or a private eye, if you can give her a job you've never seen on the screen before.

In "Sketch Artist", the hero is a frustrated painter who works as a police sketch artist. This gives him a franchise, but still makes him a regular guy. There was a series of pulp novels by George Harmon Coxe about "Casey, crime photographer", that guy who takes the pictures of crime scenes. "Striking Distance" used the Three Rivers Area river patrol, a section of the police force I'd never seen before. For years, "Quincy, MD" gave us a County Coroner who got involved in crime. If at all possible, find a franchise that hasn't been used before, instead of making your hero a cop or a private eye.

In my "Undercurrents" script, the hero is a yacht captain investigating a murder on his boat while they're hundreds of miles from the nearest port.

PAST ACTION HEROES

There are two types of hero characters in action films: the Superman Type and the Everyman Type. The Superman Type doesn't have to wear his underwear on the outside and probably can't fly.

In fact, in a recent interview with Eon Magazine, Nicholas Cage said he was interested in playing the role of Superman as an Everyman Type in the new Tim Burton film. A regular guy who dresses funny.

The Superman Type is the guy we wish we were: Tough, invulnerable, macho, action oriented. He lives in the action world, craves a good shoot out, and goes looking for trouble whenever possible. James Bond is the ultimate Superman Type. He always keeps his cool. Sylvester Stallone, Steven Seagal, and Ah-nuld always play Superman Type heroes. "Rambo" fits this category, but "Rocky" doesn't. The Superman Type was most popular in the 1980s and early 1990s in films, but has since gone out of style.

The Everyman Type is the guy we are: A normal man, vulnerable, who is forced to become involved in the action. He is a reluctant hero. He doesn't go out looking for trouble, but trouble seems to find him. Harrison Ford plays an Everyman Type in the Tom Clancy movies: A family man bureaucrat who suddenly finds himself in the middle of a war zone. Nicholas Cage was an Everyman Type in "The Rock", Kurt Russell played the type in "Executive Decision", Will Smith plays one in "An Enemy Of The State".

The Everyman Type hero has become more popular over the years, to the point of completely eclipsing the Superman Type. Though this began with Bruce Willis in the first "Die Hard", it reached a peak in "Executive Decision" when Steven Seagal was killed off so that meek-geek Kurt Russell could be the film's hero.

In the 1980s, two Everyman Type scripts designed for Richard Dreyfus were rewritten so that Ah-nuld could star in them ("Total Recall" and "The Running Man").

In today's Hollywood, the opposite is taking place. Stallone and Ah-nuld, the two most popular stars of the 1980s, are struggling to find an audience. Today's most popular stars are Everymen Tom Hanks and Harrison Ford... Regular guys, just like you and me, who are thrust into danger and have to learn how to survive. If you are writing an action script for today's audience, I strongly suggest your story feature an Everyman Type hero. Something that Harrison Ford or Tom Hanks or Nick Cage or Denzel Washington can play.

KRYPTONITE

One of the most important things to remember when creating your hero is that she can't be invincible. I recently read a script where the hero shot six armed bad guys in the opening scene. Great, but where does it go from there? In the final scene where the hero and the villain faced off in town square (it was a western) I already knew the hero was the quicker draw. Where was the suspense? Where was the conflict?

Remember, villains must always be stronger than the hero. That's another one of those important lessons.

In James Bond films, the villain is always a father figure to Bond. He talks condescendingly to Bond. When Bond points out a flaw in Goldfinger's plan to rob Fort Knox, Goldfinger already knows you can't transport that much gold by truck in a single day... In fact, Goldfinger's plan hinges on it. Bond is no match for Goldfinger at this point. He's also no match for Odd Job. In the Bond films, the lead hench is always stronger than Bond. We'll talk more about henchmen in a later chapter, but it's important to note than in every James Bond film, the villain is smarter than Bond and the lead hench is stronger than Bond. Bond is clearly the underdog.

The hero has to be the underdog. Always. The villain always has to be able to defeat the hero. Superman is stronger than anyone else in the world, but his nemesis Lex Luthor always manages to find a big chunk of Kryptonite before he embarks on one of his schemes... Making Superman vulnerable. If your villain isn't stronger than your hero, there's no challenge, no suspense, and no reason for the audience to pay $8 to find out what happens next.

MIRROR IMAGES/FLIP SIDES

Heroes and villains are frequently linked. Belloq tells Indiana Jones: "You and I are very much alike... Our methods are not different as much as you pretend. I am a shadowy reflection of you. It would take only a nudge to make you like me; to push you out of the light." and in "The Empire Strikes Back" (also written by Lawrence Kasdan) Darth gives a similar speech to Luke.

Heroes and Villains linked this way are called "Flipsides". This device goes back as far as "Manhattan Melodrama" (1934) where the gangster and the District Attorney were childhood friends. Heroes and Villains often share the same destination, but are traveling separate roads. "Strangers On A Train" actually begins by showing us two sets of train tracks merging together, then shows us two sets of shoes walking from opposite directions to the lounge car. Both men share the same desire, to kill a relative; but Bruno (the villain) will act on his desire, while Guy (the hero) realizes that murder is impolite.

Hitchcock uses flipsides in many of his films. In "Frenzy" the hero, Richard Blaney, shares the same initials as the villain, Bob Rusk... But the initials are flipped. Like "Manhattan Melodrama", Rusk and Blaney are childhood friends... only one of them is a serial killer and the other is the police's prime suspect... And the only one who can stop the killer from striking again.

I used a similar device in my script "The Base", about a disgraced Marine named Ronald L. Murphy given the assignment of infiltrating a secret society on a Marine Base. The secret society is run by the charismatic Sgt. Marty L. Rackin. Hero and villain share more than the same initials, both are searching for father figures, both have troubled pasts, neither is good at following orders, both have trouble with authority figures.

Once undercover, Murphy becomes Rackin's best friend... practically his brother. They are flipsides. When Murphy discovers that Rackin's secret society is running drugs on base (and worse), he must turn against his own surrogate brother, betray him, in order to complete his mission.

TO DESTROY HIM I MUST BECOME HIM!

Even if the hero isn't the villain's flipside, the hero often must BECOME the villain in order to conquer him. A by-the-rules cop has to go renegade ("The Big Heat") or a meek everyman must become a warrior ("Straw Dogs"), the hero usually crosses the line into "villain territory" before he can vanquish him. Often there is a physical transformation as well.

In Oliver Stone's "Platoon" Charlie Sheen's face becomes scarred throughout the film, until he resembles Tom Beringer (the villain). In "Apocalypse Now" and "Predator" the heroes paint themselves to resemble the villains before they go into battle against them. In "Predator", the creature chameleons to look like the forest; before the final battle, Ah-nuld coats himself with mud and leaves, becoming almost invisible in some shots.

In "Face/Off" John Travolta must not only take Nick Cage's face to vanquish him, he must also live Nick Cage's life!

OPPOSITES REACT

Sometimes it's not the similarities between heroes and villains, but the DIFFERENCES that are important. In "Die Hard" Bruce Willis is a hard working blue collar every day guy, and Alan Rickman is a suave tailored over educated snob. There is an underlying theme of working class struggle in "Die Hard" which links it to the social message films Warner Brothers was famous for in the 1930s, like "Captain Blood". When Willis and Rickman tangle at the end, it's working stiffs like you and me against a profit hungry corporate raider (literally).

Analyze the similarities and differences between your

hero and villain. They are the two most important characters in your script. You should know EVERYTHING about them BEFORE you begin writing. If you haven't spent the time developing their relationship you'll end up with an unsatisfying action script... And audiences won't care about the fight scenes.

IT TAKES TWO TO TANGLE

The hero and the villain will usually tangle at least three times in the course of the script. A set up in Act 1, where the hero gets stomped. A second meeting in Act 2, and the final confrontation in Act 3, where the hero kicks butt. That Act 3 confrontation is usually called the "high noon", because the hero and villain will actually face off against each other.

In Westerns and Samurai films, there is usually a highly stylized scene where the hero and villain size each other up before drawing their weapons.

"Die Hard" uses this device: there is a moment where Rickman and Willis just look at each other and laugh. Then the shooting starts.

In many action films, the hero has a PAYBACK LINE in the high noon confrontation. A payback line is a snappy line uttered by the villain to the hero in their first confrontation, which the hero "pays back" to the villain in the final confrontation.

"Die Hard" even uses a payback line in the middle of the script. After the terrorists blow up an LAPD tank, McClane grabs a walkie talkie and reasons with Hans to let the tank pull back. Hans says, "Thank you Mr. Cavalry, I'll take it under advisement", then blasts the tank again, killing the survivors. Later, when McClane drops explosives down the elevator shaft, he says "Take this under advisement, dickweed."

Audiences love packback lines. The more clever the line, the more they'll cheer. The payback line illustrates that the hero has now gained the confidence and control to vanquish the villain.

Remember, the HERO must vanquish the Villain. The sidekick or love interest can't do it, it's not their job. And the Villain can't trip and fall off a cliff or over the side of a building into wet cement (the boring non-climax of "Rising Sun").

There can be NO QUESTION about the hero being the cast member who has destroyed the villain. It's the hero's job. In "hoist by my own petard" cases, the hero must contribute to that hoisting (my apologies to Shakespeare). The villain can't trip and fall in the path of the "laser beam designed to destroy Cleveland", the hero has got to push him.

By the end of Act 3, the hero has taken a few beatings from the villain. Now, we writers are a civilized, kind hearted, nice group of folks... but the audience wants blood! They want vengeance! They want to completely destroy the villain! And the instrument they will use for that vengeance is the hero, their identification character. So, even if your hero is a pacifist monk who preaches non-violence, he's got to be the one to destroy the villain!

DESTROYING THE VILLAIN

You know how we learned in the last chapter that the bigger the villain's plan, the bigger the film? Well, add this to the list of "important things": the better the villain's death, the more satisfying the ending.

That audience that's screaming for vengeance doesn't want to see the villain go to jail. They don't want to see him sustain critical wounds and die later in the hospital. They want to see him annihilated!

The hero can't just shoot the villain, he must destroy him. The most satisfying villain's deaths involve exploding the villain into a million pieces. Gross, sure! But ask anyone who's seen "Wanted: Dead Or Alive" or "The Fury" and they'll agree.

Imagine in "Star Wars" if the Death Star had just gone dark from a power failure, instead of exploding into a zillion pieces. Kind of a let down, right?

In "Wanted: Dead Or Alive" when our hero, Rutger Hauer, finally captures the evil terrorist, he forces a hand grenade into the villain's mouth and ties a string from the pin to his hand. This prevents the villain from getting any ideas of escape. But the villain still manages to be irritating. So Hauer pulls on the string. The pin pulls out of the grenade, the villain runs away, and BLAM!

Remember, the audience has to know that the villain is dead. That means he either has to be exploded, fall off a very tall building or out of a plane, or shot up by gunfire. Too many times we have seen "dead" villains, stabbed by knives, come back to life for a few minutes of "schlock shock" action. Audiences know that if the badguy isn't in pieces, he isn't dead.

Try to come up with a clever way for the hero to vanquish the villain, but make sure you aren't stretching credibility. The hero's job is to vanquish the villain, and your job as a screenwriter is to come up with a fun, interesting, but logical way for the hero to do his job.

Once the hero's job is over, he can go back to his peaceful life as a pacifist monk; knowing that his inner and outer problems have been solved.

INTRODUCING
A CHARACTER

In your screenplay, you'll have one scene in which to introduce your lead character, before he becomes involved in the plot. The idea is to develop a brief signature scene which sets the character up for the rest of the film.

In "THE IPCRESS FILE" (1965) we see Harry Palmer wake up in the morning and prepare for a day of work. It is a simple scene which tells us EVERYTHING we need to know about this character. He has to find his glasses before he can see the alarm clock. He grinds his own gourmet coffee beans, and uses a complicated coffee maker. He looks out his flat window while drinking his coffee. Later, he finds a woman's ear ring in his bed... while searching for his misplaced gun. And he leaves his apartment late for work.

Everything we need to know about Harry Palmer is established in this scene... From here, the film whisks us away on an adventure.

The best way to write an introduction scene is to make a list of everything the audience needs to learn about your lead character. Then come up with a single scene which illustrates each of these important points in an entertaining way.

The "Hot Dog" scene in "DIRTY HARRY" (1971)

is a good example. Harry is sitting at the counter in a blue collar diner eating a hot dog when he spots a car idling in front of a bank across the street. Harry tells the diner owner to call the police, then unholsters his 44 Magnum and stops the bank robbery single handed, destroying ANYTHING which gets in his way. Finally he threatens the downed bank robber, and gives his signature line: "Do you feel lucky, punk?"

What do we learn about Harry from this scene? 1) He's a blue collar guy. 2) He's incredibly observant and smart. He sees the smoke from the tail pipe of the car parked in front of the bank, and figures out that there is a robbery in progress. 3) He carries a non-regulation gun. A HUGE gun. A gun that isn't designed to wound, but to kill. 4) He faces the robbers alone. He is fearless. 5) He doesn't wait for back up. He's a lone wolf, not a team player. 6) He continues eating his lunch as he brings down the robbers. This is just another normal occasion for Harry. 7) Nothing gets in his way on his quest for "justice". He trashes the entire block while catching the criminals. 8) He doesn't give the wounded robber the Miranda-Escobito warning... He threatens to KILL him. No kid gloves, here. This guy treats criminals like scum. 9) We learn many other details, and also get audience identification with Harry: This interrupts his lunch. Not even a sit-down lunch, but a lousy hot dog. Anyone who has ever had their lunch interrupted by work knows how Harry feels.

We learn at least nine very important things about Harry from this one brief scene. By the time Harry gets a new partner and is set out after the Zodiac Killer, we know exactly how he will react in every scene, because it was all set up in the introduction scene.

HERE'S THE INTRODUCTION of the lead character (the opening scene) from my HBO World Premiere script "Crash Dive!":

EXT. SUB COMMAND - DAY

A sign outside the building identifies it as: Submarine Command, East Coast Operations.

An aging sports car brakes to a stop in front of a 'No Parking' sign, and JAMES ALLEN CARTER climbs out, a manila folder overflowing with paper in his left hand and a cup of coffee in his right.

CARTER is USN, Ret. Even though he's on the wrong side of 40, he's still in shape. Trim, but not pretty. Unshaven, his hair windblown, and his clothes look as if he's slept in them. His coffee cup exclaims the joys of bass fishing. He jogs up to the door, careful not to spill his coffee.

INT. SUB COMMAND - DAY

Carter jogs down the hall, evading the occasional UNIFORM.

Without a word of dialogue or exposition, what have we learned about James Carter? See how I use the old sports car as a metaphor for Carter? When he parks right in front of the No Parking sign, the audience will probably laugh. We like people who break the rules. Carter is late for work, something many of us can relate to. He seems a little disorganized, but that's okay, because in the next scene we will find out that he is a technical genius who has just solved a problem in 27 hours that the best brains at MIT couldn't solve in three months. Twenty pages later, the United States will be threatened by nuclear blackmail, and bookworm James Carter will be dropped behind enemy lines to use his photographic memory to save the world. Unfortunately, the bad guys have guns and knives...

Another way to intro your character is the reveal. This is a second person technique, where we find out about your character through the dialogue or actions of others, then meet her.

The dialogue method is frequently used in Westerns. A group of grizzled cowboys sit around a poker table, talking about the meanest, toughest, fastest, gunslinger in all the west. Each contributes a story showing a different side of this gunslinger. "He once shot eight men without a reload. That bullet bounced from one man to another like a billiard ball." "I once saw him tear a man's arm clean off in a fist fight." "I personally know he ruined three of the girls at Miss Kitty's... They went and fell in love with him afterwards and quit the business." "The army put him in Yuma Prison once, but he tunneled his way out with his bare hands." "That's nothing, I heard some of Metaxas' raiders took him out to the middle of Death Valley, shot his horse, and left him to die. Only it backfired. He walked out of that desert and hunted every man to a one down. Shot them dead. One guy he shot in the kitchen in front of his wife and kids." "He's a tough one, that Roy Slade." As soon as the audience gets a vivid picture of who this desperado is, the saloon doors open and THERE HE IS... Woody Allen in a cowboy hat!

The main problem with introducing a character through second person dialogue is that it's talking heads, and film is a VISUAL medium. Show, don't tell.

So the visual second person intro is the one we most often see. Three examples:

One. In Ben Hecht's "Notorious", we see a wild party in progress. Dancing, drinking, people going into the coat room to make love. Amidst all of this carousing, we see a man sitting in a chair, back toward us. This man turns down all invitations to dance. He isn't drinking. He seems very businesslike. With every invitation he turns down, our curiosity about him GROWS. Finally, the hostess (a provocatively dressed Ingrid Bergman, looking HOT!) tries to force him out of his shell. No success. As the party dies down, she continues flirting with him. Nothing. Now we REALLY want to know what this guy's game is. Why is he even at this party? He is after something, but what?

Soon, it is only Ingrid, a passed out drunk, and the mystery man. She makes a pass at him, he turns her down flat. He only wants to talk to her. We FINALLY dolly around to see the Mystery Man's face... It's Cary Grant. Our hero. In this scene, we find out many things about Grant's Devlin character, most important is that business comes before pleasure in his life.

In fact, he is so business oriented that we wonder if he ever has ANY fun. Certainly, he has no love life. We also learn how focused he is, how easy it is for him to avoid temptation, and how patient he is... Like a hunter waiting in a duck blind for hours until the prey takes flight. All of these elements will figure into the story. Some of them will be assets, other liabilities.

Two. "Raiders Of The Lost Ark" has a similar reveal character intro. We are POV of the guides, cutting through a jungle. Who is leading? Not a guide, but our lead character. We only see the back of his head. When the expedition comes across something scary in the jungle, the guides pull back in terror... Our lead continues forward. When we come upon traps, our lead avoids them, but the guides (who are indigenous to this area, and should KNOW what to do) fumble and get killed. After we've learned how brave, crafty, gung-ho, intelligent, relentless, independent, and strong our lead character is, we see his face: Harrison Ford as Indiana Jones.

Three. I used a combination verbal and visual reveal in my "UNREASONABLE FORCE". We take the POV of a Homicide Detective at the crime scene. As the Detective comes up to each member of the MCSU Team, they say something which tells us about the Detective. A Uniform Cop is reverential, showing that the Detective is powerful. A Fingerprint man makes jokes, showing that the Detective has a sense of humor. The ME tells the Detective that the victim is a close range shotgun blast, really messy, then lifts the bloody cloth covering the corpse so that the Detective can see. The Detective isn't squeamish. Each person the Detective comes into contact with gives us another clue to who the Detective is. We develop this image of a tough, competent, action oriented cop... Then twist around to reveal pretty single mom Kelly Brooks. After the reveal, Kelly talks about the inconvenience of finding a sitter at short notice in the middle of the night. Couldn't these people get killed at a reasonable time of day? When babysitter rates are cheap? In one scene, we learn everything we need to know about Kelly Brooks, so that the audience has a good idea how she will react in the rest of the film.

Whether your character is a tough cop or a single mom (or both) it is important for you to familiarize the audience with your lead character quickly and succinctly, so that they may settle into their seats and enjoy the rest of the film. Create a character introduction scene early in the script, and pack it full of information. Then let the story take control, and take the audience on a roller coaster ride for the rest of the film.

ORGANIC ACTION

Every once in a while I see a movie where all of the pieces don't seem to add up. About a dozen years ago, Harry Hamlin was in a film titled "King Of The Mountain". It was about car mechanics who race cars on L.A.s twisty Mulholland Drive (where Jack Nicholson lives). Suddenly, about twenty minutes into the film, there's a scene with a rock band practicing. For three and a half minutes, the entire audience scratched their heads, wondering who these people were. The film took another ten minutes or so before connecting the band to the racing mechanics... You see, the singer was Harry Hamlin's girlfriend.

What did she have to do with car mechanics? Racing Mulholland Drive? And why do we need to see her do four songs in the course of the film?
Unfortunately, there are no answers to these questions. They needed a way to pad the script, and tossed in this subplot.

It seemed as if the writer wrote plot ideas on a deck of 3 x 5 cards, then sailed the cards from across the room into a hat. Zoom, a miss! Zoom, another miss! Click, a hit! When he had five cards in the hat, he wrote a script with those five plots. None of the ideas added up, or connected to each other. That script was full of fertilizer! (my Mom might be reading this).

My dictionary defines "Organic" as "being grown without added chemicals or fertilizer". Another definition is: "constituting a basic part: integral".

So ORGANIC SCREENWRITING is telling a story where all the parts are integral, and there's no bull shit (sorry, Mom). Everything in the script is connected to a single "plot seed", and grows directly from that seed.

Plot GROWS from character.

There went half of my readers! There are two schools of structure: Internalists (like John Truby) and Externalists (like Michael Hauge). "My Guru's better than your Guru!" Well, I'm a member of neither camp. My definition of "story" includes the philosophies of BOTH schools.

WHAT IS A STORY?

"STORY" is the point in a character's life where he/she is forced to confront and solve his/her inner conflict in order to solve the outer conflict."

This ties the inner conflict to the outer conflict.

Which means OUTER CONFLICT will change depending upon which character is your lead. One character's story will have a different crisis point than another character's story.

"Joe" and "Cathy" are married. Joe's crisis point might come after five years of marriage, but Cathy's might have taken place before she ever met Joe. If we tell Joe's STORY, Cathy is a part of it, but if we tell Cathy's STORY, Joe is no longer a character in your script.

So put aside all of your plot information until you figure out who your lead character is, and what their inner conflict is. Some of your plot work may be unusable, if so, file it away for another script. Don't try to force a plot or a scene into the wrong story. It'll end up looking like fertilizer.

ORGANIC EXAMPLE

In John Michael Hayes' script for "Rear Window" the STORY is Jimmy Stewart's fear of committing to Grace Kelly. He sees his life as dangerous and hers as glamorous. He not only can't imagine her in his dangerous world, he wishes to protect her from it.

Every character in the film, including extras and walk ons, all talk about their marriages and relationships; specifically, the compromises required between vastly different people. EVERY character in this film is a reflection of the Stewart/Kelly conflict.

The OUTER CONFLICT is Stewart's growing belief that Mr. Thorwald across the courtyard has murdered Mrs. Thorwald in order to end their marriage. The Thorwald's are vastly different people. Mr. T (like Stewart) travels for a living (Thorwald's a salesman, Stewart's a war photographer). Mrs. T (like Kelly) is confined to one place (Mrs. T is an invalid confined to her bed, Kelly is a fashion model confined to the New York fashion world).

The INNER CONFLICT meets the outer conflict when Stewart must ask Kelly to enter his dangerous world in order to solve the murder across the courtyard.

Notice how much time Stewart spends trying to get his policeman friend to investigate so that Kelly won't have to. When she finally goes into "Stewart's world" and searches the Thorwald apartment (as Stewart bites his nails across the courtyard), she finds and WEARS Thorwald's wife's WEDDING RING. Is this a coincidence? Could it have been an ear ring? (No!) The wedding ring is symbolic. It not only proves that Stewart need not be afraid of dragging Kelly into his dangerous world, but that she could be a good marital partner (That symbolic wedding ring).

The film ends with Stewart and Kelly together, and obviously committed to each other.

INNER CONFLICT?

"Wait a minute!" some of you are saying. "IN-NER CONFLICT? Hey, we're talking about ACTION pictures, aren't we? We don't need no stinking Inner Conflict!"

Without an Inner Conflict your lead has no character arc. He or she becomes two dimensional. Cardboard. The audience will have trouble identifying with your lead, and find the over-all conclusion of the film less satisfying. Sure, you might be able to get away with not having an Inner Conflict with the 'Superman Type' lead character, but why would you want to?

As a challenge, I've taken an existential action film from the 1960s, "Point Blank" starring Lee Marvin. The lead character has almost no dialogue and shows no emotions... But he has an Inner Conflict!

The plot: Lee Marvin plays Walker, a career criminal who cooks up a large scale robbery with the help of his wife and best friend. After pulling the heist, the wife and best friend kill Walker and split with the cash. But Walker rises from the dead, tracks them down, and kills them and anyone else who gets in his way. A cold hearted vengeance machine. The character arc: Before the robbery, Walker is a playful, fun, character. We see him flirting with his wife, joking with his best friend. He's alive. After he's shot, he becomes cold and brutal. Dead inside. Unfeeling and uncaring.

He hooks up with his wife's sister (played by Angie Dickenson) and uses her to find both his wife and best friend. After both are dead, Angie accuses him of being dead inside. Of not caring or trusting anyone.

The Inner Conflict: Walker has his vengeance, but still isn't satisfied... he wants his cut of the robbery money, and drafts Angie to help him. Angie fights him, and Walker finally realizes he will have to trust her and care about her, or she isn't going to help him. He must heal himself and stop being dead inside in order to achieve his goal.

Conclusion: After he rejoins the living and learns to love and trust again, he has the strength required to get his cut of the money... But realizes he can be satisfied without it. He's alive again! Walker is forced to confront his Inner Conflict (being dead inside) in order to solve his Outer Conflict (getting vengeance and his stolen money back).

THEME AND NEXUS

The OUTER CONFLICT is tied to the INNER CONFLICT. It grows naturally and seamlessly. And where the inner and outer conflicts connect, we have the THEME.

When the inner and outer conflicts are connected, the theme can be explored visually (through actions rather than words).

The NEXUS is where the inner and outer conflicts

connect with each other.

In my script, "THE LAST STAND", a mob accountant turns state's evidence. After testifying, he goes into Witness Relocation, and begins a new life with his wife and son in suburbia. Three years later, the mob finds him, and asks him to go back to New York for a "mob trial". If he doesn't go peaceably, they'll use force.

The accountant must turn against one FAMILY (the mob) to protect another FAMILY (his wife and son). Throughout the script are various scenes and examples of "Protecting The Family". All of the characters are defined by their families. The MOB is a family. The POLICE are a family. The FBI is a family. Each family tries to protect its members.

The second NEXUS in the script is in the title. The accountant TAKES THE STAND to testify against the mob. The mob wants him to come back to New York to TAKE THE STAND in a mob trial. And when he refuses, he has to TAKE A STAND against the mob's violence. His home becomes the LAST STAND (like Custer's) in his gun battle with the mob. In fact, the hero has TAKEN A STAND to protect his FAMILY.

It all ties together.

I made lists of words and phrases which described the INTERNAL conflict and a list for the EXTERNAL conflict. Then I looked for Nexus words and phrases. The dialogue is peppered with double meaning lines: People who talk about the external conflict, but describe the internal conflict.

Every scene in the script has to do with the hero and his family. Some scenes are the "mob family" and some are the wife and son. In second draft, I went through the script and cut out every scene which didn't involve the family. Those scenes were fertilizer.

WHERE INTERNAL AND EXTERNAL MEET

Once you've found your "PLOT SEED", that inner fear your hero doesn't wish to confront, you create an external plot which will force him to confront it. The external plot MUST GROW naturally from the hero's quest to solve his inner problem. The Villain's Plan will also grow from that Plot Seed, and will involve the very thing our hero most fears.

BY THE NUMBERS

Here is a standard recipe for an action script (feeds six) which shows the relationship between internal and external conflict. After doing hundreds of Timelines of my favorite action films, I noticed a pattern emerging, and here it is:

In the first 10 pages of the script, the hero and his INTERNAL problems are introduced. His internal problem has left him "broken" somehow. He is just going through the motions of life. Around page 10 (or earlier) we hit our first plot point.

The next 20 pages set up the EXTERNAL problem. The villain strikes, leaving the hero faced with a physical problem which must be solved. A problem which can only be solved by facing his inner fears.

At the 30 page point (end Act 1) is a MAJOR change in the plot. Something happens which pushes our hero off a cliff so that he MUST deal with the external problem. For the next 25 pages, our hero tries to solve the external problem while avoiding the internal problem (his fears). He slaps band aids on the problem and tries the quick fix. But none of this works, and he falls deeper into the Abyss.

At the MIDPOINT (page 55) the hero realizes that he can't solve the external problem without confronting the internal problem. He reaches an EMOTIONAL CRISIS, because his entire life is based on avoiding his internal problem (his fears).

The next 25 pages thrust the hero into increased danger from his external problem. There are a few close calls where he's almost killed. Finally he reaches his "Popeye Point", where he's had alls he can stands and he can't stands no more.

Around page 80, our hero confronts his fear head on. By this point, he realizes that if he doesn't confront his internal fear, his external problem will KILL HIM. Given the choice, he faces his internal fear, doing the very thing he most hates. The result is, the part of him which was "broken" is now repaired, and he can function at full force.

Act 3 begins with our hero as a new (whole) man. In action films our hero usually gears up for battle to show that he is ready to take on the EXTERNAL CONFLICT head on. Donning war paint and loading his guns. The next 25-30 pages of the script pits our stronger hero against the villain, in a series of escalating actions, until the villain is destroyed.

Act 3 ends with a few pages of our hero, as he

returns to his normal life as a stronger, happier person, no longer living in fear. His EXTERNAL PROBLEM has been solved and his INTERNAL FEAR has been overcome. Also, he usually gets to kiss the girl.

ORGANICALLY GROWING
YOUR ACTION SCRIPT

Start with your "plot seed": the internal conflict of your lead character. Something in his past he doesn't want to face. Some deep fear. Some mistake he's made and never gotten over.

In "Vertigo" we see Jimmy Stewart's fear of heights causing the death of his policeman partner. The fear of heights is tied to his partner's death.

From that fear grows the plot. Because the plot will force our hero to face his fear.

ORGANICALLY GROWING A HIT FILM

In "Breaking Through, Selling Out, Dropping Dead" (one of the best common sense books on the film biz), William Bayer explains why some films are hits and others are flops.

"A picture becomes a hit when the fantasy it represents coincides with the needs of the audience." A hit film explores a subconscious fear or desire currently held by the audience.

This explains why a cheap action programmer like "Death Wish" becomes a box office smash. At the time "Death Wish" came out, people felt that the court system wasn't working, and that they were powerless against crime. "Death Wish" explored a fear the majority of ticket buyers were feeling. It was a HUGE hit.

About three years ago, there were a bunch of news stories about moms re-entering the work force; concerned about the quality of day care, and that the day care workers were seeing more of their children then they were. You could make a hit film by tapping into these subconscious fears. The tool you use is...

MAGNIFICATION

Magnification takes a minor problem that we've all experienced, and exaggerates it all out of proportion.

Begin with the plot seed. In this case, our hero's fear is: What do I really know about the people watching my child? Does my child like their day care supervisors more than they like me? And are my children safe?

MAGNIFY the story. Instead of a TV drama about child care, blow the problem up into a thriller. We aren't dealing with a day care worker who beats your child, we're talking about a nanny who wants to MURDER your child. We aren't dealing with your child becoming attached to the nanny, but a nanny who's breast feeding your baby when you aren't looking!

Using the organic method, your plot seed grows into an exciting, heart pounding thriller which addresses a major fear in the subconscious of the audience. Because it addresses this subconscious fear or desire, it becomes a huge hit, and makes millions of dollars (even though it cost two thirds less than the average film). You might call your script "The Hand That Rocks The Cradle".

With Magnification you can use a problem we've all dealt with in an entertaining, larger than life story. And all grown from a single "plot seed". No fertilizer!

Give it a try with your action script, and see what you can grow! Maybe a sleeper hit like "Death Wish" or a blockbuster hit like "Die Hard".

POINT OF VIEW

One of the central tools a novelist uses is the ability to jump back and forth between characters, showing each of their points of view. Heroes, villains, love interests, and even minor characters like bellboys, maids and taxi drivers may be given center stage in the story for a few scenes. Stephen King goes so far as to jump into Cujo's point of view in the novel which bares his name, and give us a dog's eye view of the story.

One would think that film, with its ability to jump from place to place, time to time, and character to character, would be even freer with it's point of view... And one would be wrong.

Beginning screenwriters (and even some old pros) often try to take their script from character to character, examining each point of view...

And completely losing the focus of the story.

Remember, story is character in conflict. Not a PLATOON in conflict, not a FAMILY in conflict, not a CITY in conflict. All of these are basically abstracts. If you are doing an ensemble piece about five friends who get into trouble, each one of the five will handle the trouble differently. That's FIVE stories. It is difficult enough to tell ONE story in two hours. Splitting the focus of your film five ways is the road to disaster.

A good example of this pitfall is the film "Quiz Show" written by Paul Attanasio. Despite good reviews, great acting, and the publicity machines at Disney working around the clock to promote it, "Quiz Show" never caught on with audiences. Why? Because it lacked a SINGLE POINT OF VIEW.

Audiences couldn't figure out if it was an underdog story about John Turturro, an intellectual Rocky, who fought poverty and discrimination to become a national celebrity on the 21 Show.

Or was it a detective story about reporter Rob Morrow digging out the corruption behind America's most popular television program?

Or was it the tale of a wealthy but not particularly bright Faust, who sells his soul to the Devil in exchange for the love of his father?

These are three interesting stories, and if the script had only chosen ONE to focus on, they would have had an exciting and engaging screenplay. But with the audience constantly shuttled back and forth between points of view like an orphaned child, we were unable to fully immerse ourselves in any of the three stories. As soon as we began identifying with the John Turturro character, we were yanked out of that story and shoved into the Ralph Fiennes tale.

The protagonist in one story is the antagonmist in another. Are we supposed to like Rob Morrow or hate him? Is Ralph Fiennes a good guy or a bad guy? We are never really sure who we are supposed to root for, because the script's point of view keeps changing.

I'm not advocating the disuse of subplots, nor am I saying that the lead character must be in every scene. Scenes featuring the love interest, or the antagonist, or the sidekick are all perfectly acceptable. But when you can't tell the sub plot from the main plot, or become unsure as to who is the protagonist and who is the sidekick, you will lose the audience.

The MAJORITY of the scenes in your script should feature the protagonist, and the central plot of the script. All subplots and sub characters should be subservient to the lead character and her or his conflict. When a producer asks you what your story is about, you should be able to tell him in one sentence, which describes ONE character involved in ONE conflict. When they read your script, that single sentence should describe every scene in it, as well as the whole 110 pages. Each scene illustrating the conflict, plus adding to the overall conflict.

The most successful films take the audience on a journey: The lead character's journey. Through identification, the audience will BECOME the lead character, and see the story through her eyes. Feel the lead character's joys and terrors. Participate in their life for two hours. You can't take the audience on a journey if it involves too many trains (of thought), all going in separate directions.
So choose your lead character. Choose her conflict. Focus your script on a single journey, which this lead character must take in order to deal with their conflict. If your story is focused to the central character's point of view, it will be easy for the audience to hitch a ride. Scripts are ultimately written for your audience, so don't lose sight of them while typing. They're out there. On the other side of your computer screen. Waiting for an adventure.
Remember, the journey of a thousand miles, begins with two words: FADE IN.

BONUS TECHNIQUE!

"The Minor Mischief Trick"

Audiences love rogues who bend the rules. People who do the things we wish we could do... if we only had the guts. We can use this to create likable characters without using some corny "pet the dog" scene.

Your hero loves jelly filled donuts (except for those sour lemon ones). Someone brings a box of donuts to work, one for each employee. Your hero grabs a filled donut, takes a bite... it's lemon! Yech!

In real life, we'd have to eat the whole donut. But your hero waits until no one is looking, then replaces the donut, carefully concealing the bite taken out of it, and grabs another donut. The audience smiles; we wish we could do that!

In "Conspiracy Theory" Mel Gibson is a taxi driver who can't find a parking place. A car has taken two parking places... So he uses his cab to push the car out of the way, creating a parking space. We instantly like him. It's wrong, it's illegal, but it serves that parking space hog right, doesn't it?

In one of my scripts, the hero has no parking meter change. So he pulls a parking ticket out of his (overflowing) glove box, puts it under his windshield wiper. Great trick, huh?

THE TWITCH

Film is a visual medium, which requires stories told in pictures. Deeds not words. But good stories need their protagonists to wrestle with inner demons, to overcome inner fears, and to solve inner conflicts. How do we display a character's inner conflict on screen without thought balloons or voice overs? I use a method which I call "The Twitch".

A "Twitch" is a physical manifestation of a character's internal conflict. A symbol of the conflict which the character can refer to throughout the script. An icon, a fetish doll.

The term comes from the "Pink Panther" movies. Whenever Clouseau's name was mentioned around Herbert Lom's character, he began twitching uncontrollably, exposing the way he felt about Clouseau. Without saying a word, we understood Lom's thoughts and emotions. Though you might be able to get away with something like this in broad comedy, in a drama, action film, or other genre; reality and subtlety are called for.

A Twitch is always a physical object: a photo, a medallion, a watch, a cane, a hat, a ring. It differs from a Touchstone, which is a symbol used to remember peaceful, regular life when the character's world has gone to hell. The cliche Touchstone is the family photo a soldier looks at when under fire in a fox hole. The most famous is a sled called "Rosebud".

Probably the funniest Touchstone ever devised was in a sketch on the old Carol Burnett Show. Harvey Korman played a soldier about to go off to war who asks Carol for "a little something to remember her by" (sex?). Carol responds by giving him a HUGE potted plant from her living room. He vows to keep it close to his heart. The rest of the sketch was the standard WW2 soldier in a foxhole drama, with the ludicrous giant potted plant never leaving Korman's hands as bombs blast all around him. No matter how bad the war became, he still had that potted plant.

A Touchstone is a physical object which brings calm to a character. A Twitch reminds the character of an unresolved conflict.

In Robert Rodriguez's "Desperado", the Mariachi's musical career ends when his girlfriend is murdered and he is shot in the hand. Whenever he picks up a guitar, he is reminded of his girlfriend's death. The guitar is the Mariachi's twitch. It symbolizes the death of his girlfriend, the death of his career, the death of his dreams. When the little boy asks him to play, he only manages a few notes before the pain overwhelms him. The guitar, which was once the Mariachi's source of joy, is now his source of pain... And the use of the guitar case to hide his weapons is further symbolic of his inability to let go of his rage and need for vengeance. The film is filled with guitars and guitar cases, all symbolic. When he meets a new love, a new source of hope, she gives him a guitar as a gift. At the end of the film, he throws his guitar case of weapons as far as he can, removing the pain.

There are two types of Twitches, Early and Late.

THE LATE TWITCH

The best examples can be found in the Spaghetti Westerns of Sergio Leone. In "Once Upon A Time In The West", Charles Bronson plays a character known as Harmonica. He is never seen without his harmonica on a lanyard around his neck. Through out the film, a great deal of mystery is built up around the harmonica. Why does Bronson always play it in the presence of the steel eyed killed played by Henry Fonda? Why is it Bronson's most important possession, something worth dying for? Bronson spends a great deal of time touching the harmonica, studying it. The harmonica is clearly Bronson's twitch, symbolic of.... something.

The mystery builds until the end when the mystery is revealed in a flashback: The Steel Eyed Killer puts a noose around Bronson's father's neck, then hoists him onto young Bronson's shoulders. Then he uses the harmonica to gag young Bronson's cries for help. Young Bronson gets tired (and begins breathing rapidly on the harmonica) and collapses, his father hangs. When Bronson faces the Steel Eyed Killer in a gun battle as an adult, he shoots the man who killed his father... Then places the harmonica in the killer's mouth so he can hear his own last breaths.

One of the most famous Late Twitches are the musical pocket watches from Leone's "For A Few $ More". Colonel Douglas Mortimer has a pocket watch which he frequently studies. The villain, Indio, has a musical pocket watch which he uses the tune to time gun battles. Indio seems haunted by his watch, and as the film progresses, we see snippets of a flash back, getting the history of the watch a little at a time. A woman gets the watch as a gift. Indio kills the woman's husband. Indio rapes the woman. The woman kills herself rather than be raped. Indio takes the watch from the dead woman's hand. At the end shoot out between Mortimer and Indio, we finally see the Colonel's watch: It's the same as Indio's. The raped woman was Mortimer's sister, and the Colonel has been on a mission of vengeance.

The Late Twitch was recently used in Sam Raimi's homage to spaghetti westerns, "The Quick And The Dead".

THE EARLY TWITCH

This is the method I prefer. You give your protagonist a physical object with personal meaning. In a 'tell scene' (usually in act one) the protagonist explains the significance of the object. From that point on, whenever the protagonist touches the object, it reminds the audience of the protagonist's history. Like the guitars in "Desperado" or the silver bracelet in Borden Chase and Charles Schnee's classic western "Red River".

In my HBO World Premiere movie "Virtual Combat" I needed a way to remind the audience that Quarry was tracking the villain because his partner was killed (partially due to Quarry's negligence). So I had Quarry snag a photo CD of his partner from his personal effects. This becomes Quarry's twitch, a reminder of his involvement in his partner's death. He carries it throughout the entire script, consulting it often. Once it's established, whenever he brings it out, the audience knows he is thinking about his partner and his own failure to save him.

A similar twitch was used in "Strange Days". Ralph

Fiennes keeps CD ROMs of his old lover. The film's best scene has Angela Bassett throwing them to the floor, breaking them, and telling Fiennes to forget the past and get on with his life.

In my script "Undercurrents" a sailor named Jeff takes a job captaining a yacht for a husband and wife con-man team. He becomes involved with the wife, Nola, and the con game. In so deep he doesn't know what's real and what's part of the charade. Jeff wears an old compass on a lanyard around his neck. Here is the 'tell' scene:

                    NOLA
          What's this?

                    JEFF
          Compass. My father gave it to me when I was
          ten.

                    NOLA
          Really?

                    JEFF
          Every couple of months, he'd save up enough
          money to rent a boat for an hour, and take
          me sailing on Lake Merritt.
                    (beat)
          A stupid little two man boat. We would sail
          around to the amusement park and sail back.
          That's all we had time for.

                    NOLA
          An hour of sailing is better than none at
          all.

     Jeff takes the compass from her hands, studying
     it.

```
            JEFF
He was an alcoholic. Used to spend all night
drinking, and wake up not knowing where he
was.

Jeff rubs his thumb over the compass.

            JEFF
I always know where I'm going. Where I'm
going to wake up.

Nola presses her body against him, lips close.

            NOLA
I NEVER know where I'm going to wake up.
It's more exciting that way.

Their lips blend and passion ignites them.
```

The compass has become more than a directional device, it symbolizes Jeff's fears of aimlessness, his fear of becoming like his father, his fears of confusion. It is a symbol of his lack of self confidence. The compass has become his crutch, and he touches it frequently.

When the story takes some unexpected twists and turns, Jeff finds himself completely lost. The compass is broken, taking away his sense of direction. He doesn't know what's real, or where to turn. He looks at the broken compass for a clue, but it gives no answers.

Only when he has learned to trust his own instincts, to navigate by 'dead reckoning', is he able to discard the broken compass and take charge of his life.

Whenever Jeff touches the compass, the audience knows he is "lost" without a word of dialogue. After the tell scene it has become a symbol for Jeff's internal struggles, his fears and lack of confidence. When he finally discards it, we KNOW he has conquered his inner conflict and is ready to take on the world.

THE DOUBLE TWITCH

In Jeb Stuart and Steven E. deSouza's "Die Hard", Holly Genero is given a gold Rolex watch by her employers. This Twitch symbolizes her allegiance to career. Her husband, John McClane, has spent the entire film realizing he must admit he's been "a jerk" and meet her halfway. The antagonist Hans, a terrorist/"exceptional thief", is motivated by his greed.

During the fight scene at the end, Hans is pushed out a window, but grabs hold of Holly's watch band, almost pulling her out with him.

As Hans dangles 30 stories above the ground, holding tightly to the symbolic gold Rolex, Holly makes a decision: To cast off her single minded quest for career advancement and meet her husband halfway. The watch band is opened, and Hans holds tight to the gold Rolex as he falls to the ground.

The Rolex is a double twitch: It symbolizes Career to Holly, and Greed to Hans. By using the Twitch, Stuart and deSouza have added shading and irony to a scene where a villain falls out a window to his death. Imparting the most information with the least amount of verbiage. That's what Symbols and Icons are all about.

My cable film "Black Thunder" has an interesting variation on the Double Twitch. The ultimate Stealth Fighter plane is stolen by terrorists, and Air Force test pilot Vince Conners is brought in to get it back. Conners was trained by the best, a gung-ho "Right Stuff" test pilot named Tom Ratcher, now retired from the Air Force. Whenever Conners gets into the cockpit of a plane, he tapes a photo on the control panel (Conners' twitch). The photo shows Ratcher with one arm over Conners' shoulder. But the photo is cropped so that we can't see Ratcher's other arm.

To get back the stolen Stealth Fighter plane, Conners is partnered with his rival and worst enemy, Rick Jannick. In the past, Jannick's hot-dog attitude almost got Conners killed.

Late in the film, Jannick is captured by the villains. They go through his belongings, and find a photo (Jannick's twitch). The photo shows Jannick's mentor, Tom Ratcher, with one arm over his shoulder...

The other third of Conners' photo!

The full photo gives the audience Conners and Jannick's back story: They were rivals for Ratcher's fatherly affection. Because Conners was Ratcher's favorite, Jannick was forced into his crazy hot-dog attitude to get attention. The same photo is not only both Conners and Jannick's twitch, it is also the key to their relationship.

An Early Twitch for Conners which becomes a Late Twitch to explain his relationship with Jannick.

CYMBALS AND SYMBOLS

YOUR TWITCH OBJECT must be chosen carefully, as it's appearance will have great meaning.

If your script is a story about a love affair which begins to sour, have the couple win a heart shaped helium balloon at a carnival in an early scene. Then, as their love begins to fade, the helium balloon gradually sinks to the floor and deflates. Every time we see the balloon floating a little bit lower, we KNOW the love between our couple is diminishing.

Since the object is symbolic of the character's internal conflict, it should obviously relate to that conflict.

In my "Hot Sheet" script, my protagonist is an ex-pro football player whose career and plans for the future are shattered along with the cartilage in his knee. He's out of the game, and finds himself without a future. Giving up on life, he begins a hermit-like existence as the owner/manager of a run down beach front resort. His cane is the constant reminder of his knee injury, and his lack of future.

As the story unfolds, he begins to see an a new future for himself, and becomes less reliant on his cane. Every time he experiences a minor drawback, he grabs his cane for support. Finally, he reaches a crisis point where he must confront his inner fears. He must decide if he is a used up cripple, or a man who will fight for himself. He throws the cane away, and stands tall. No longer a victim.

If I tried to express this in dialogue, it wouldn't work. It would come out corny and pretentious. And film is a medium of actions, not words.

Tossing aside a cane is a hard image worth a thousand words of dialogue.

THE TEMPORARY TWITCH

There are times when you don't want to show the inner conflict of a character, but just give us a peek at his or her emotions. That's when the temporary twitch is useful.

In William Goldman's "Marathon Man" Dustin Hoffman has had a very negative dental experience. He uses a vial of oil of cloves to deaden the pain in his teeth. When he makes the decision to take on the badguys himself, he throws the vial to the ground, shattering it. Now we KNOW he's ready for action.

In my script "High Impact" a father is searching for his kidnapped son. I needed to find a way to show that each was thinking of the other, when they were separated my many miles.

So I used a temporary twitch.

Just before the boy is kidnapped, the father breaks a Hersheybar in half to share with his son. Because they are about to eat dinner, both put the halves of the candy bar in their pockets for later. Then the son is kidnapped.

As the son is held captive, he breaks off sections of the Hershey bar... and we KNOW he's thinking of his father.

As the father searches frantically, the only food he has is the Hershey bar, which he eats a section at a time, thinking of his son.

With hundreds of miles separating them, they are together. Joined by the Hershey bar. When each gets down to the last of their six sections, each separately chooses not to eat it. To keep the section as a reminder, to be eaten together.

Whether you use a Twitch early or late, or just to illustrate a temporary emotional state, it is an important tool with which to show the inner emotions of a character without resorting to dialogue.

A way to tell the audience what a character is thinking without voice overs or speech balloons.

A way to use pictures instead of a thousand words.

ACTION IS ACTION

Why are Action Films popular the world over? Why are the top international stars Schwarzenegger, Eastwood, Jackie Chan, and Stallone? Because Action is something we can SEE. It translates into any language. Remember, the literacy rate in Zimbabwe is only 30%; which means 70% of the audience can't read the subtitles. But everyone can follow he action.

Film is a VISUAL medium.

Hitchcock said; "Rely on action to tell your story, and resort to dialogue only when it's impossible to do otherwise". In a drama, people argue; in an action film, they fight. A scene here a man asks a woman for a kiss and she turns him down isn't as cinematic as a scene where a man steals a kiss and the woman SLAPS him.

In films we SEE events happening. That's the most important screenwriting lesson there is.

Action scripts aren't "talking heads". A scene where two cops sit at the police station and discuss their case is boring. Let's SEE them find the clues, search a suspect's flat, or canvas a neighborhood. Let's SEE them run down a clue that proves useless.

DIALOGUE IS EVIL!

Hitchcock again: "Silent pictures were the purest form of cinema." The idea of any movie is to tell a story in pictures. This does not mean to direct on paper. You shouldn't be writing camera angles, or film and stage directions. But you should be writing stories which are VISUAL in nature and are about people doing things.

Watch a commercial for a national product. In 30 seconds, they have to tell you a story and sell you a product. Usually there is little or no dialogue. Just images, and a narrator telling you the name of the product. Fragrance and car commercials often skip the narration entirely. Isn't it amazing how some commercials manage to tug at your heart strings? There was an appliance commercial a few years ago about a husband and wife at a family function who bump into each other on the stairway of their home and fall in love all over again. Not one word of dialogue, but a MAJOR emotional impact.

Would you like a good screenwriting exercise? Grab a camcorder (if you don't own one, borrow one) and unplug the microphone. Draft a couple of friends to act. Now script and film a little movie which tells a complete story with NO dialogue and NO narration. All you have are pictures. You'll have to concentrate on what the audience SEES, not what they hear. You will learn more about telling a story visually by this exercise than you would by taking a dozen script seminars. Make one of these little movies every six months, and you'll find yourself continuing to learn.

Another way to learn is to watch films which were international hits. Like "Road Warrior" or "Aliens".

Let's study "Road Warrior": Rent it tonight and count the lines of dialogue. Don't count the opening narration, which was designed to bring those who'd missed the first Mad Max film up to date. You'll notice there is almost NO dialogue in the entire film. Most of it is chases and fights.

My favorite scene is when the leader of the gas-makers gives his big speech about what their society stands for. He gets about three words out of his mouth when we pan over to Max, who's unfastening his handcuffs... The rest of his speech is unintelligible background noise to a silent scene where Max tries to escape and is caught by the Feral Kid.

That's the film's big dialogue scene. It runs almost three minutes, but all we hear are a few words.

Is "Road Warrior" a fluke? No. Rent "Planet Of The Apes" or "Aliens" tomorrow night and count the lines. Or grab the script to "Die Hard". Sometimes the script goes as long as three pages without a single line of dialogue. It's all action. Just like the movie.

TALK, TALK, TALK

When I read action scripts by novices, the biggest error is too little action and too much talk.

I recently read an action script where most of the action took place off screen. Police were tracking a criminal, but they always ended up at the crime scene after the action was over. They'd stand around the dead body, sipping coffee and talking about the case. Then they'd go to the police station and talk about the case. We'd cut to the criminals, as they sat around their hide-out talking about how the police were closing in on them.

Finally, after 95 pages of talking, the police caught up with the criminals. Six pages of "Come out with your hands up"/"You won't take me alive." and "The reason why we killed them was...." Then a half page shoot out, maybe six gunshots total. The badguy's bullets missed, the cop's bullets all found their mark. 102 pages of script, maybe one page of action.

How would you feel if you paid $8 to see this 102 minute Harrison Ford action film, and there was only one minute of action? The rest was just Harrison sitting around talking? Would you be angry? Would you want your money back? Would you tell all your friends the film was a waste of time? Would you recommend the film to a friend? Now, if you were a studio reader, would you recommend that your company spend $70 million to make this script?

Action films have to be filled with action. That's what they ARE. Action scripts aren't dialogue scripts. You can't write: "There is a big car chase, and the villain's car explodes." That's boring. The trick of writing a good action script, is to fully describe your action scenes in ways that are exciting to read. Action scenes need to be thrill a minute page turners, where the reader can't wait to find out what happens next. The average studio reader comes to a block of action and wants to skim it. Your job as a writer is to make them read every single word, then skim the dialogue to get to your next action scene... Just like what YOU do in the theater.
Have you ever rented an action video and fast forwarded through the dialogue scenes to get to the next fight or chase? I have. "One Man Force" starring the late John Matuszak. Great action scenes, bad acting and silly dialogue. It's a "finger on the search button" special. You just can't wait to get to the next action scene. That's how your script should be!
How do you write exciting action passages? Use reversals, suspense, ticking clocks, rug pulls, and twists !

REVERSALS AND RUGPULLS

Shane ("Lethal Weapon") Black says: "The key to a good action scene is reversals. The "Star Wars" movies work because they are FULL of reversals." What's a reversal, you ask? Let Shane explain: "It'slike a good news, bad news joke. The bad news is, you get thrown out of an airplane. The good news is, you're wearing a parachute. The bad news is, your rip cord breaks. The good news is, you have a back up 'chute. The bad news is, you can't reach the cord. Back and forth, just like that, until the character reaches the ground. He's gonna die... no, he's not... Reversal, reversal, reversal."

JUST WHEN YOU THOUGHT IT WAS SAFE

Reversals make your action scenes unpredictable and exciting. It's one cliffhanger after another, and the audience stays on the edge of their seats wondering what will happen next.

In "The Fugitive" Harrison Ford as Richard Kimble is being chased down the stairs by Agent Gerard. Kimble reaches the lobby, but Gerard is right behind him. Kimble breaks through a crowd of people, and sees the automatic exit door only a few feet away. But the doors are whooshing closed. Gerard is right behind him. Kimble squeezes through the doors... but his foot gets stuck!

Gerard draws his gun, and gets ready to shoot. Kimble tries to wiggle his foot out. Gerard takes aim. Kimble squeezes his foot out of the door. Gerard fires! Kimble hits the dirt. Gerard re-aims. Kimble stumbles to his feet. Gerard has a PERFECT shot and squeezes the trigger. BANG! The glass scars... it's bullet proof. Kimble gets away.

For a really good example of reversals, rent "El Mariachi" by Robert Rodriguez. The film's TOTAL budget was only $7,000.00 so there was no money for special effects, stars, or locations. The only thing Rodriguez had was the script, and he filled it with reversals.

My favorite from the film is the scene where our hero is being chased down the street by armed killers and comes to an intersection. The light is against him. The killers are gaining. Our hero grabs the tailgate of a passing pick up truck and flips inside the bed. The killers get to the intersection and see the pick up truck zooming away. Our hero breathes a sigh of relief... he's safe!

The villain gets on his walkie talkie and tells his henchman that he hero has escaped in a truck, can the henchman head him off? In the pick up truck bed, our hero ducks down so that no one can see him. The henchman tells the villain: "I don't need to head him off. He jumped in the back of MY pick up truck. Want me to bring him around?" The hero panics as the pick up truck swings around and takes him BACK TO THE VILLAIN!

EVERY action scene you write should have reversals in it.

The best way to create a reversal is to look for the road less traveled. In any scene, there are at least two choices. Pick the one you've never (or seldom) seen.

Then think "good news, bad news".

What if the villain has a 13 shot Browning and the hero has a 5 shot Smith and Wesson? You're setting up a reversal, by having the hero run out of bullets (at a critical moment, of course). When the hero finally gets the villain in his sights and pulls the trigger... CLICK! Bad news. Then, let's say, the villain raises his gun. Worse news. But the hero THROWS his empty gun at the villain, hitting him in the face. Good news! The villain shakes it off (he's REALLY macho) and reaims. Bad news! Now keep it going for an entire action scene, and you'll create a page turner that no reader can skim.

PLOT TWISTS

REVERSALS are little twists which occur within a scene. If the twist takes the STORY in another direction, it's a "plot twist". The most common criticism of beginner's scripts is that they're too predictable. The reader KNOWS what's going to happen next, so why read on?

Already, you're up against the conventions of the genre in making your script unpredictable: We KNOW the hero will win and the villain will be vanquished. So our job as action writers is to make sure the story DOESN'T take a direct path from beginning to end, but corkscrews a little.

In William Goldman's "Marathon Man", Babe's brother dies in his arms after being murdered by the villain. His brother's partner/lover, Janey, asks if his brother said anything before he died. Any important information? Babe says "No". Later in the film, Babe has been kidnaped by Zell, who asks the same question... Only Zell is using a dentist's drill to jog Babe's memory. Suddenly, Janey breaks into Zell's secret hide-out and rescues Babe. As they speed away, Janey asks Babe what he told Zell. "You've got to tell me."

After Babe answers, Janey turns the car around and takes him BACK to Zell's hide-out! Twist!

Janey is a badguy! When we look back on this twist, it makes perfect sense. From the very beginning, Janey was trying to find out what Babe's brother told him. The "rescue" only makes sense if Janey is a badguy. How else would he have known the location of Zell's secret hide-out?

That's the most important rule about twists: They have to be logical upon reflection. In this video age, audiences can actually rewind the tape and look for the clues to the twist. If they aren't there, they'll cry "foul!"

The clues to the twist are called "Foreshadowing", and they are REQUIRED for every twist. Plant the clue to your twist as early as possible, to give the audience lots of time to forget it. That way, after the twist occurs, they'll remember the foreshadowing and say to themselves: "I should have seen it coming!"

Be careful when foreshadowing your twist that you don't "Telegraph" it. You want the audience to find the clues AFTER the twist, not BEFORE it (or it isn't really a twist). This is a balancing act which takes some practice before you'll perfect it.

The best twists are completely unexpected when they happen, but logical upon reflection.

There's a good twist in Ernest Lehman's "North By Northwest". Cary Grant is chasing a man named George Kaplan, who is (in turn) chasing James Mason (the villain). Grant hops on board a train bound for Grand Rapids, Michigan (Kaplan's destination). On the train he meets Eva Marie Saint, who is also bound for Grand Rapids. They have an affair. When the train reaches Grand Rapids, Eva Marie Saint lures him into a trap! She's James Mason's mistress! One of the villains! It's a great twist, that holds up to logical examination. We know that the hero and the villain have the same destination. The train travels to that destination. We are given a clue: We KNOW that the villain is on the train. The only thing we DON'T know, is that the villain and Eva Marie Saint are in cahoots.

Twists have to be logical, and twists have to be IN CHARACTER. If the sidekick suddenly turns out to be the villain's henchman; there had better be character nuances and a planted back story to explain it... Even then, I'm not sure the audience will buy it.

DO YOU BELIEVE IN MAGIC?

The best way to create a twist is through "magic". A magician uses DIVERSION and ANTICIPATION to trick the audience. When a magician shows you that there's nothing up his sleeve, he is secretly pulling a card from the secret pocket in the back of his coat and sliding it under a glass of water on the table. You have focused your attention on his sleeve... and it's a diversion. For the remainder of the trick, you anticipate that the card will appear in the hand at the end of that sleeve, and are completely surprised when the card turns up under a glass of water on the table.

A TWISTED EXAMPLE

There's an old Hitchcock Presents episode about a guy who gets pulled over by the police on his way home from work. The guy says "I know I was speeding, but can you give me a break? It's my birthday, and my wife's making a special dinner." The cops put him in handcuffs. "We aren't arresting you for speeding... we're arresting you for MURDER." Our hero says there must be a mix up, he's innocent. "They're ALL innocent." The hero PLEADS. It's his birthday. His wife is waiting at home. "You've got the wrong man." One of the policemen shows him a sketch of the killer... and it's our hero! Now our hero begins to panic. It's his birthday. Things like this aren't supposed to happen on your birthday. Our hero again pleads innocence. The mean policeman says, "That's it. We WERE going to take you to the stationhouse, but NOW we're going to take you to an old warehouse and beat a confession out of you." Our hero really panics when the police car turns into an industrial section and pulls up in front of an old warehouse. He PLEADS. "I'm innocent. Don't beat me!" The policemen drag him into the dark warehouse and flip on the lights. "Surprise!" It's a surprise birthday party thrown by his wife and friends!

When you look back on this episode, you realize that the surprise party is the logical thing to happen on our hero's birthday... getting arrested for murder isn't.

The arrest was a DIVERSION from the surprise party. When the policemen take him into the warehouse, we ANTICIPATE it's because they want to beat a confession out of him. Boy, are we surprised! This twist works because the LOGICAL COURSE OF EVENTS (the surprise birthday party) is the twist.

When we hold the diversion up to the light, we see just how flimsy it is: What are the odds that someone who looks JUST LIKE YOU committed a murder? What are the odds that the cops would spot you driving around and arrest you for the murder? And don't these cops seem a little hasty to beat a confession out of a guy who cooperates with them? The entire arrest scenario isn't logical... but we believe it because the writer focused our attention away from the real story. He tricked us, just like a magician.

That's the way to create a good twist: Focus the audience away from the logical progression of the plot through diversion and anticipation... then, when the logical events occur, it's unexpected!

RUGPULLS

A rugpull is like a twist to the 100th power. A rugpull is a MAJOR twist which shocks the audience and takes the plot in an entirely unexpected direction.

A good example is the "Psycho" shower scene. What's shocking about that scene isn't the nudity or the graphic violence, it's that the LEAD CHARACTER is killed. The audience doesn't know what to do. They've never been presented with a problem like this in a movie before. The hero isn't supposed to get killed one third of the way through the film. It just ISN'T supposed to happen that way!

A rugpull is DRASTIC. Although I wouldn't recommend killing your lead character (that's TOO drastic), killing the sidekick, the love interest, or the lead's mom UNEXPECTEDLY is a good rugpull.

Neil Jordan's "The Crying Game" has a great rugpull. The film's famous secret takes the story into such a strange and unpredictable direction, that the audience doesn't know what will happen next. You might at first think that this is just a twist, but twists don't make the audience jump that high out of their seats, nor will a twist change the entire course of the story and characters. After that rugpull, NOTHING in "The Crying Game" is the same. Even when the IRA gunmen come back into the story, the plot has derailed onto such a different track that the outcome isn't what you thought it would be.

In my "Hot Sheet" script, I offered this rugpull. The set up: Wright (the villain) believes that Mack (our hero) and Trish (Mack's girlfriend) have stolen three million dollars in drug money from him. Wright has given Mack 24 hours to produce the money, or he will return with his sadistic henchman, Jack... and time has just run out...

EXT.   MOTEL POOLSIDE - NIGHT

Wright snaps his fingers and Jack yanks Trish out of the lounge and holds his 44 Magnum to her head.

Mack tries not to panic as Jack presses the gun into her hair.

                    WRIGHT
          I want my money.

                    MACK
          I don't have it.

                    WRIGHT
          He'll kill her if you don't give me the
          money.

```
          MACK
I don't have it!  You've gotta believe me!
I was gonna take it, but it was gone when I
got there!  You've GOT TO believe me!

          WRIGHT
I believe you.
```

Wright turns to Jack and nods.
Jack pulls the gun out of Trish's hair.

Mack sighs in relief.
So does Trish. The tension is over.

Then Jack pulls the trigger, blowing Trish's brains
all over the chaise lounge. BLAAM!

Her corpse drops into the pool with a splash.
Mack takes off running. He is chased by gun fire.

After a rugpull, ANYTHING is possible.

The audience has been hit by something so unexpected that they don't know what will happen next. You could kill the hero. The victim might still be alive. The villain might even win! A word of caution: Rugpulls are like nuclear weapons. You can't use them indiscriminately. You can't use them in every script. You have to hold on to a rugpull, and only use it when you have no other choice. I've written sixty scripts, and only about a half dozen have rugpulls.

TWISTS, REVERSALS, and RUGPULLS keep the pages turning on your script, and keep the audience interested in what happens next. A good twist will have the audience jumping out of their seats and screaming.

But to keep the audience on the EDGE of their seats, we fill our scripts with suspense.

BONUS TECHNIQUE

"Hold Your Twists"

The longer you "hold" a plot twist, the more powerful it becomes.

EXAMPLE: In my script "Unreasonable Force" a pair of Detectives are ambushed by a gang. One Detective is shot in the chest and goes down, the other barely escapes with his life. The gang torches the police car and the corpse inside. The survivor feels guilty. He should have helped his fallen partner instead of run. What if his partner had still been alive at the time?

The surviving detective has to tell his partner's child that Mommy isn't coming home... she was killed in the line of duty.

The surviving partner sinks into depression...

Not knowing that his partner is alive! She was wearing her bullet proof vest. The body burned beyond recognition in the police car is a female gang member shot in the cross fire.

The longer you give the audience to accept that the partner is dead, the greater the impact of the twist when they find out she's alive.

They get used to her being dead. They come to accept it as a fact... THEN you spring your twist!

SUSPENSE

Keeping the audience on the edge of their seat is the function of SUSPENSE. Suspense is not the same as action, nor is it the same as surprise. Suspense is the ANTICIPATION of action. The longer you draw out the anticipation, the greater the suspense.

Hitchcock explained; "Two men are having an innocent little chat. Let us suppose that there is a bomb underneath the table between them. Nothing happens, then all of the sudden, BOOM! There is an explosion. The audience is surprised, but prior to this surprise, it has been an absolutely ordinary scene, of no special consequence.

"Now let us take a SUSPENSE situation. The bomb is underneath the table, but the audience knows it... Probably because they have seen the villain place it there. The audience is aware that the bomb is going to explode at one O'clock, and there is a clock in the decor. It is a quarter to one. In this situation, the same innocuous conversation becomes fascinating, because the audience is longing to warn the characters on the screen: 'There's a bomb beneath you, and it's about to explode!'

"In the first case, we have given the audience fifteen seconds of SURPRISE at the moment of the explosion. In the second case, we have provided them with fifteen MINUTES of SUSPENSE."

There are two basic kinds of suspense: the "ticking clock" (or time lock) and "cross cutting". The Hitchcock example above is a ticking clock. We are given an event which will occur at a certain time, and our suspense builds as time passes.

You can further divide 'ticking clocks' into two categories: Big Clocks and Scene Clocks.

THE BIG CLOCK

The big clock is a ticking clock which covers the ENTIRE film. A major event in the film will occur at a certain time, and the hero is usually racing to stop it... but time is running out. A good example of The Big Clock is "High Noon". We know the bad guys are arriving at noon, and suspense builds as every minute ticks away. In "High Noon" that grandfather clock becomes the focus of the film, and we keep returning to it.

As every minute ticks away, Will Kane comes closer to the big shoot out. Kane tries everything to get help, and as time ticks away, he becomes more desperate... and the audience becomes more involved.

Another classic western uses a big clock in the exact opposite way. In "3:10 To Yuma" (based on a story by Elmore Leonard), our hero is a regular guy, a farmer, picking up some spare change guarding an evil desperado in a hotel until the 3:10 prison train comes to take him away. In "High Noon" the clock is ticking away until the confrontation begins, in "3:10 To Yuma" the clock ticks away until the confrontation is over. If our hero can hold off the desperado's henchmen until 3:10, he'll survive. But the henchmen's plans escalate as time passes. Becoming more and more violent. After a while, we begin to wonder if our farmer-hero can survive the attacks by these evil gunslingers. If he can hold on just another ten minutes.... That's suspense!

A good example of The Big Clock can be found in Stephen DeSouza's "Commando". John Matrix has twelve hours until the plane he was supposed to be on lands and the villains realize that he has escaped. That's twelve hours to find and rescue his kidnaped daughter... or the bad guys will kill her. Matrix sets his digital watch to count down the hours, and he frequently glances at his watch to find out how much time he has left.

As the film goes on, time ticks away until we're down to SECONDS before they kill his daughter.

The Big Clock is what separated this film from the dozens of other throw away action films, and ended up making Arnold a star.

SCENE CLOCKS

If there's a MACRO there must be a MICRO, and 'Scene Clocks' can also be used to create suspense. A Scene Clock is like the Hitchcock bomb. A small ticking clock used in a scene or a series of scenes to keep the movie hopping.

A good example of the Scene Clock is the nuclear bomb used at the end of "Goldfinger". Goldfinger activates the bomb, then handcuffs James Bond to it. Toss in Odd Job as a diversion and you've upped the suspense through cross cutting (which we'll get to later). After Bond fries Odd Job, he races to the nuclear bomb, with time ticking away. He tries to disarm the bomb, but what does he know of nuclear weapons? Tick. Tick.

Tick. Minutes left to seconds left. Then the nuclear expert arrives and begins the disarming procedure. But is there enough time left? Tick. Tick. Tick. The seconds run out. We SEE the timer clock, as it goes from double digits to single digits. Tick. Tick. Tick. The bomb is finally disarmed with only SECONDS to spare.

(Trivia question: How many seconds?)

Whether it's a Scene Clock or a Big Clock it's based on a DEADLINE. A certain EXACT time when something is going to take place. The more EXACT the time, the better the suspense. If your villain says "I'll be back at nightfall to kill you", it's not as effective as if he says "I'll be back at seven fifteen to kill you". We can look at a clock and SEE how many minutes are left until seven fifteen, but looking at the sky and trying to figure out when nightfall starts is open to interpretation.

The sooner the audience knows that deadline, the sooner the suspense begins. And the more often we SEE the ticking clock (some physical manifestation of time passing) the better the suspense. Have the hero look at his watch, have him run into a store with a clock...

We have to KNOW how close the deadline is.

DOES ANYBODY KNOW WHAT TIME IT IS?

But you can also use the LACK of a physical clock to build suspense. Have you ever been on your way to work and got caught in a traffic jamb? No watch and your car clock doesn't work? You KNOW you're late for work, but you don't know HOW late. So you keep searching for a clock. Maybe the bank has one? No. Maybe you can see the clock in the 7-11 store. It's too far away, you can't read it. I've had this happen to me, and become so desperate to know what time it is that I've looked through the windows of cars to try and read other driver's watches.

I decided to use this idea in a recent script called "Hard Return" after hearing my friend Roger Ebert constantly complain about how overused those red LED bomb timers are in films. The world as we know it will be destroyed in ten hours. A big red LED "countdown clock" on the wall of Mission Control begins counting back - 00:59:59 - 00:59:58 - 00:59:57 - Counting the seconds until we are all dead. Then the power goes out.
Instant panic.
"Does anybody have a watch?" Someone has an old fashioned watch, but has it been set for the right time? Is the sweep second hand accurate? Wait, is that minute hand on the seven or the eight? What if it's two minutes off, and the world ends before we complete the mission? I took the cliche red LED timer and turned it!

WHEN TIME RAN OUT

No matter how you use the clock, time MUST be running out. The less time left on the clock, the higher the suspense. Obviously, if the villain's bomb is set to explode in an hour, it's more exciting than if it's set to explode a week from next Tuesday.
Don't stop with one clock. Use multiples. A Big Clock and a few Scene Clocks. You can't have too much suspense.
In "The Satan Bug" (a classic suspense film from the 1960s) a villain has stolen germ warfare stuff from a top secret government lab.
The Big Clock has our hero trying to figure out

who the villain is and where he has the germs stashed before the villain escapes. There are a half dozen Scene Clocks, ending with the hero capturing the villain and the villain explaining that he's planted a germ bomb in Los Angeles set to go off at noon.

That final Scene Clock keeps the last twenty minutes of the film hopping as the good guys try to find, then disarm, the bomb before it explodes and infects everyone in L.A. with a killer disease. It's a suspense textbook... Finally available on video.

CROSS CUTTING

The other way to create suspense is through cross cutting. Cross Cutting began as an editing technique in the silent era, designed to heighten suspense. There are two types of cross cutting, 'Action' and 'Suspense'.

For an example of 'Suspense' cross cutting we go back to Hitchcock: "A curious person breaks into someone else's room and begins to search through the drawers. Now, you show the person who lives in the room coming up the stairs. Then you cut back to the person who is searching, and the audience feels like warning him: 'Be careful, someone's coming up the stairs!' You cut back and forth between the searcher and the flat owner. The closer the flat owner gets, the more exciting the suspense. Soon the audience is yelling, 'Get out! Get out!'"

My erotic thriller, "Riptides", is about a husband who strays while his wife is away. The husband is in bed with his girlfriend when the wife returns early from her business trip.

INT.   THE BEACH HOUSE - NIGHT
In the bedroom, Robert and Sandi make love.
Robert hears a car pull up and stops.

> SANDI
>
> Don't stop.

EXT.   BEACH HOUSE DRIVEWAY - NIGHT
Laura parks her Mercedes in the driveway and gets
out.

INT.   THE BEACH HOUSE - NIGHT
Robert and Sandi continue making love.

EXT.   BEACH HOUSE DRIVEWAY - NIGHT
Laura pops open the trunk, pulls out her luggage.

INT.   THE BEACH HOUSE - NIGHT
Robert and Sandi's breathing is ragged and loud in
the quiet bedroom.

EXT.   THE BEACH HOUSE
Laura slides her key into the front door lock.

INT.   THE BEACH HOUSE
Robert stops, listening to the sound of the keys.

> ROBERT
> (whispering)
>
> My wife...

> SANDI
>
> Don't stop.

IN THE LIVING ROOM
Laura opens the door and enters the house, setting
her luggage in the entrance hall.

> LAURA
>
> Robert?

She moves deeper into the house... To the bedroom.

Do you get the idea? Suspense cross cutting moves back and forth between two subjects, with suspense building as the two subjects become closer to each other. Whether this is a man searching a house while the homeowner gets closer, or a killer stalking a victim hidden in the closet of an old dark house, or two trains on the same track racing towards each other; cross cutting takes two people or objects we DON'T want to see in the same scene and puts them on a collision course. Suspense cross cutting can be used in a scene, or stretched over an entire script; as in "Lonely Are The Brave".

ACTION CROSS CUTTING

Action cross cutting takes two SEPARATE actions and divides the audience's loyalties between them. The idea is to create a pair of different actions, and just as one scene gets exciting, jump to the other. When that scene becomes exciting, jump back to the first scene. Suspense is created through CLIFFHANGERS at the end of each segment.

The Villain aims his gun at the Hero and gets ready to pull the trigger... Cut to the Sidekick fighting with the Henchman on the roof of a building. The Sidekick gets in a few punches, then the Henchman knocks the Sidekick off the roof! The Sidekick grabs the edge of the roof with his fingertips. The Henchman steps on his hand... Cut to, the Hero drops to the floor just as the Villain fires. The Hero rolls across the carpet and knocks the Villain down. The gun goes skittering. The Hero scrambles for the gun. The Villain grabs a table and swings it at the Hero's head. The Hero aims the gun at the Villain and pulls the trigger. Click. Out of bullets... Cut to, the Sidekick...

The audience wants to find out how the Hero gets out of his problem AND find out how the Sidekick gets out of HIS problem. By cutting between the two, you can draw out the action, and draw out the suspense, for quite a few minutes.

Action Cross Cutting works great in Act 3, where you have to fill 20 pages with exciting action sequences. It allows variety and suspense, and keeps the reader turning the pages to find out how the hero gets out of THIS one. But the reader can't skim, or she'll never find out how the Sidekick survives.

Suspense is the backbone of every film script, no matter what genre. Comedies, romances, science fiction, westerns, and of course, Action Films.

By using ticking clocks and cross cutting, you can keep those pages turning, and keep the audience glued to the edge of their seats. Remember, folks, we're in the bladder bursting business!

SECRET SUCCESS

"It's a film with a secret." How often have we heard those words? When we hear them, don't we want to run right out to the theater, plunk down our $8, and find out what that secret is?

When it comes to writing successful action screenplays, I've got a secret. Do you want to know what it is? Of course you do. Everyone loves finding out a secret. It makes us feel naughty and superior at the same time.

You still want to know my secret? What if I DON'T tell you? Wouldn't you get angry? No need to worry.

My secret is.... Secrets! I use them in my scripts, and you can, too. Secrets can be divided into BIG SECRETS, LITTLE SECRETS, and CHARACTER SECRETS.

BIG SECRETS

Big secrets are usually found in mystery films, but have been put to good use in such dramas as "Suddenly, Last Summer". A big secret helps drive the film. The audience either knows about the secret, and is on the edge of their seat hoping no one will discover it; or are trying to discover what the secret is, given various hints and clues throughout the story.

My favorite Big Secret is from Robert Towne's "Chinatown". Evelyn Mulwray is protecting her husband's alleged mistress. Why? There is some connection between the two women, and we spend much of the film wondering what it could be. Usually wives and mistresses don't much care for each other (with the exception of the two in "Diabolique").

The curiosity gets the best of detective Jake Gittes, and he forces Mrs. Mulwray into a confrontation. By this point, the audience is more than just curious. We KNOW this is some huge deep dark dirty secret. We've been waiting the entire film to hear this. We KNOW she is about to reveal the one thing she has never revealed to anyone. And we get to eavesdrop!

Evelyn admits that the mistress is her sister... And her daughter. That her father molested her and she had a child by him. This is a secret so shocking, audiences were talking about it months later. To be in on a secret this big is delicious! The reveal of this secret becomes the crescendo of the film.

It becomes apparent on a second viewing, that the Big Secret is what has been driving this film almost from the beginning. The moment the mistress is introduced, the question on every character's mind is: Who is she? The quest for her identity becomes the focus of the script. With every scene, our curiosity grows more intense, until the final reveal.

A variation on the "Chinatown" Big Secret was used in Carl Franklin's "Devil In A Blue Dress". But the secret was not given enough power in this script. The film should have focused on the question: Why would a beautiful white society woman enjoy hanging out in the all-Black South Central Los Angeles? Then when that big reveal comes in act three, it would have the same impact as the reveal in "Chinatown".

The secret of using Secrets is to come very close

to revealing the secret (without doing so) several times within your script. To bring up the secret constantly. To ask the question "Why would a wife protect her husband's mistress?" or "Why would a white society woman hang out in a Black neighborhood?" Since you can't actually ask the question more than twice in your script, your character's ACTIONS must lead the audience to ask the question themselves.

Evelyn Mulwray isn't curious about her husband's mistress, and actually pays Jake to forget about her. Later she hides the mistress. Most of Evelyn's ACTIONS in the film are aimed at keeping her relationship with the mistress a secret. Every time she lies to Jake about the mistress, we ask ourselves: "What does she have to hide?" The more you can get your audience to ask that question, the more impact the reveal will have upon them.

Big Secrets may also be found in all of Tennessee Williams' Southern Gothic plays, like the aforementioned "Suddenly, Last Summer" which has a big secret which includes homosexuality, cannibalism, and private beaches.

LITTLE SECRETS

Little Secrets can take a bland scene and turn it into an intense, nail biting, edge of the seat experience. Where Big Secrets drive a story, Little Secrets drive a scene. A Little Secret is something, which if discovered, will place our protagonist in hot water. The audience is usually let in on the secret at the beginning of the scene, then we sit on the edge of our seats hoping that no discovers it.

A great example of a Little Secret appears in Steven de Souza and Jeb Stuart's screenplay "Die Hard". John

McClane is battling terrorists (lead by Hans Gruber) who have taken his wife Holly, sleazy businessman Ellis (and others) hostage in a high rise office building.

If the terrorists learn the relationship between McClane and Holly, they will hurt her to get at McClane.

A VOICE comes over McClane's radio.

>   HANS VOICE
>   I have someone who wants to talk to you. A
>   Very Special Friend who was at the party
>   with you tonight.

McClane's face falls. Oh, God. Eyes closed, he waits for the voice that tells him it's all over.

>   VOICE
>   Hello, Johnny Boy?

McClane's eyes open, showing equal parts shock and hope.

IN THE OFFICE

Camera adjusts to show ELLIS as Hans gives him the CB.

>   McCLANE
>   Ellis?

Ellis has a cigarette, and a Terrorist brings him a diet coke.

>   ELLIS
>   John, they're giving me a few minutes to try
>   and talk some sense into you...

>   McCLANE
>   (carefully)
>   Ellis, what have you told them?

```
                    ELLIS
      I told them that we're old friends and you
      were my guest at the party.

McClane sighs, partially relieved.
HANS, meanwhile, narrows his eyes.

                    McCLANE
      Ellis... you shouldn't be doing this...
```

This scene builds suspense around the secret of John McClane's identity. The audience knows he is Holly's husband. That is his point of vulnerability. This secret must be hidden at all costs.

When the scene begins, McClane and the audience think that Hans has discovered the secret. Then when Ellis speaks, we think Ellis may have told the secret.

When we find that he hasn't told the secret, we begin to worry that the terrorists will FORCE Ellis to tell the secret. Knowing that a secret EXISTS is a partial reveal. Even if the terrorists completely believe Ellis (they don't) they will want to learn details about McClane.

Each detail is a stumbling block, which may reveal the secret. Every word Ellis speaks is another step closer to Hans discovering that McClane is Holly's husband. Another step closer to Holly's torture or death.

I used a Little Secret in my Made For Cable movie "Hard Evidence". A businessman is framed for murder, and realizes the only way out is to plant the murder gun and other evidence on the real killer. The murder evidence (and three quarters of a million dollars in blackmail money) are in a briefcase. As the businessman gets ready to meet the real killer (and plant the evidence) there's a knock at his door. The police Detective investigating the crime! Then a very tense scene occurs where the businessman is questioned by the Detective with the briefcase full of evidence sitting on a table between them. The Detective places his hands on the case several times in the scene. Once he even plays with the latches. Each time, you think he might discover the evidence and arrest the businessman. What could have been a typical "Detective questions suspect" scene becomes an edge of the seat nail biter because of the inclusion of a secret. The audience wants to scream "Don't let him find that!" at the screen.

Little Secrets can also be used for comic effect. Watch any episode of "I Love Lucy" for an example. In every scene, Lucy is trying to hide a secret from Ricky, and comedy grows from the exaggerated lengths to which she goes in order to protect her secret. How many chocolates can you hide in your mouth?

Including a Little Secret in almost every scene will create tension, suspense, (or comedy), and identification with the protagonist in your audience. The secret becomes the sub focus of the scene. A counter point to the dialogue, and a way to expose character.

CHARACTER SECRETS

Character Secrets are the stuff Southern Gothics are made of. Dark, personal, family secrets which must remain hidden at all costs, only to be unleashed in a volcanic explosion of drama at the end. Though Character Secrets fuel the works of Tennessee Williams and Lillian Hellman, they need not be the stuff of explosive drama. Because what separates Character Secrets from Big Secrets is: Character Secrets need not be revealed in the script. They can remain secrets.

I am positive some are now asking, "What is the use of having a secret if it is not revealed? How will the audience ever know of it's existence?"

A secret helps define a character and create a subtext for his or her actions. What we feel we have to hide from others tells us a lot about ourselves. Maintaining that secret will influence every choice we make. Every choice our characters make.

Let's say we have a businessman who inflates his resume in order to land a job. Now this businessman lives in fear that the lie on his resume will be exposed. He may lose his job. He also begins to see himself as a fraud.

Do others in his firm wonder why he seems to have less experience than his resume boasts? Do they begin to think of him as second rate? Will our businessman compensate for this by being overly punctual and bureaucratic? Or will he work extra hours in hopes that if his secret is discovered, his job performance will outshine it? Or does he become a delegator: Giving tasks which may expose his weakness/ secret to others? He may become the office paranoid, living in constant fear that others are trying for his title.

Quite a lot of characterization choices from one fudged resume, eh? This secret shades what might have been a standard businessman, turning him into someone three dimensional and different. Someone with a secondary motivation in every scene. Hide the secret. Make sure no one discovers it.

Before writing a script, I usually write a biography for each of my characters. Included are such mundane things as weight, eye color, parents' names, education, first love, worst job, pet words and phrases, and anything else which I may need to refer to while writing the script. But I also include the character's "dark secret", which may be anything from an inflated resume to something larger and more gothic like incest or murder.

I usually don't reveal the dark secret in the script, but it tints the dialogue and actions of every scene that character plays in.

Big Secrets, Little Secrets, and Character Secrets are splendid tools for creating character, drama, suspense, or humor within a screenplay. One of my favorite Southern Gothic secret reveals is in Gene Wilder's wonderfully funny screenplay "Young Frankenstein". Frau Blucher has been hiding a dark secret for the entire film, and when pressed by Victor, she reveals it in a huge dramatic scene by proclaiming her relationship to the mad Baron Frankenstein: "He.... He.... He... was... my.... Boyfriend!"

SECRET SUSPENSE

Secrets are like little ticking time bombs, waiting to go off. Waiting to twist your tale into a new direction or fuel your characters to make dangerous decisions.

Secrets are part of your life, and they should become an integral part of your character's lives. As was noted in Stephen Sondheim and Anthony Perkin's brilliant screenplay "The Last Of Sheila": "The harder you try to keep a secret in, the more it wants to get out."

If you have a secret, everybody wants to know what it is. If your script has a secret, the Producer will keep turning pages, hoping to discover it. Now it's a shared secret between you and the Producer. And the harder the Producer tries to keep the secret, the more he wants to spill it to the world. On screen. In Technicolor.

So using secrets in your action script may be your secret weapon for success. I've got a secret.

ACTION GAGS

Action scripts are filled with ACTION SE-QUENCES, and action sequences are filled with ACTION GAGS. No, action gags aren't funny; they are the actual step by step pieces of an action sequence. The "gag" part is stuntman slang for a stunt. Remember, every time you write a car chase, fist fight, or shoot out; that scene will either be performed by stunt doubles, or by the stars under the supervision of a Stunt Coordinator. The stunt coordinator's job is to make the stunt look dangerous to the audience, but be safe for the participants.

A stuntman friend once told me that there are only five basic stunts.

A) HIGH FALLS: See the beginning of "Lethal Weapon" for an amazing high fall. "Stick" also has a great high fall at the end.

B) FULL BURNS: When you light a guy on fire, and the flames engulf him, that's a full burn. There are enough fire stunts in "Backdraft" for a dozen films.

C) CAR STUNTS: Car crashes, car rolls, high speed chases, holding onto the roof of a speeding car, etc. "Bullitt" has a great car chase, and "Hooper" has some unusual car stunts.

D) HORSE FALLS: Westerns have made a come-back, and brought horse stunts back with them. Anything that has to do with horses falls into this category... But biker flicks use the same stunts, they just substitute a Harley for the horse. Basically, this category contains any time a stuntman falls from a speeding vehicle, be it animal or machine.

E) FIST FIGHTS: From bar room brawls to kung fu scenes. These stunts often include breaking glass, as when a bottle is broken over someone's head or that someone is thrown through a window. There's a GREAT bar room brawl in "The Parallax View".

My friend Art Camacho is one of Hollywood's top fight choreographers. His job is to cram a fist fight with so many individual gags that the audience is constantly excited. As screenwriters, we can make Art's job easier by coming up with some great gags and putting them in the script. Remember, action scenes must be fully described... but not boring. So come up with some great, exciting action gags for your script.

What I do is keep lists of gag ideas. I have one for car chases which includes every idea for a car chase I could come up with. On the sidewalk. Through an enclosed shopping mall. Down stairs. Through a building. Jumping from one roof top to another. The wrong way down the freeway. On railroad tracks with an on-coming train. Sure, you've seen some of these before, but the idea is to brainstorm up a "menu" of car chase ideas which you can use later. Work at coming up with different, unusual ideas; things we HAVEN'T seen before. I have lists for car chases, shoot outs, fist fights, foot chases, and a list for weird gags which don't fit in any category.

While American films often use the same stale action gags in film after film, Hong Kong action pictures always use some new and exciting action gags. From the amazing choreographed shoot outs of John Woo films like "The Killer" and "Hard Boiled" to the amazing stunts of Jackie Chan in "Operation Condor" and "Project A: Part 2", Hong Kong style action is always the most imaginative. Now that Hong Kong has reverted to Chinese rule, many of these writers, directors, and performers are trying to adapt their techniques to American films. But their best work is still subtitled.

To open your mind to action gags, go out and rent "Jackie Chan's Police Force" or "First Strike!" or "Operation Condor" tonight. Chan is an International star who has finally caught on the in the USA. He's a daredevil who does his own (highly dangerous) stunts, and always tries to top whatever he's done before.

"Police Force" has hundreds of action gags, from a car chase THROUGH houses (and down a hill) to an amazing sequence when Chan jumps out a (glass) window onto an awning, which RIPS, sending him falling onto ANOTHER awning, which RIPS, sending him onto a half dozen other awnings, each one ripping, but slowing his descent until he gracefully lands on the sidewalk beneath the building.

I created an exciting action gag after seeing Jackie Chan in "The Big Brawl" a few years ago. In "Big Brawl", Chan fights a pair of bad guys with a wooden bench; using the legs to hit them, and the seat as a shield. I used that gag as a base, but used a kitchen chair instead.

Using a chair as a weapon gave my hero a lion tamer feel. He could hit someone with the legs, use the seat as a shield, and pin a villain against the wall using all four legs. From that gag, I added a few flips, with the chair as the fulcrum, and ended up breaking the chair over the villain's head. Later, the villain gets the drop on our hero, and he uses a broken chair leg as a club.

When I wrote the scene, I studied a chair in my dining room and tried to figure out every single way it could be used as a weapon. Once I had a dozen "chair fight gags", I wrote my scene.

I've done other scenes with standing floor lamps as weapons (sword / bo / lance / club / and a dandy electric cattle prod after the bulb breaks) and fist fights in unusual places (elevator / roof top / bathroom / in a speeding car / kitchen / on a boat). The fist fight in the speeding car had gags based upon what you would find in a car, like the cigarette lighter and seat belts (great for strangling!). Let your imagination run wild!

Once you've filled your action sequences with dozens of interesting, fresh, action gags; your script will be so much fun to read that producers will fight over who will get to make it. Include all five types of stunts, and you'll have a stuntman's dream script.

Action gags may not be funny, but they sure are FUN. They're the cornerstone of every action sequence.

SOMETHING EXTRA

The difference between a good script and a great one is in the details, and with Producers wading through 40,000 scripts a year, your script better be GREAT. The way to make your script jump to the top of the pile is to give the audience something extra... A neat idea or device they haven't seen before. Something to talk about, after the film is over and the credits are rolling.

Here's a scene we have seen a million times before: The cops are outside the badguy's house, ready to break down the door. Guns ready, wearing bullet proof vests or riot gear. The cops always wonder what's behind that door. When they break it down, will they find an army of bad guys waiting to shoot them down? Will they find a mother and her child, and realize their informant has given them the wrong address? Or will they find their suspect alone and unarmed?

The question for the screenwriter is, How do we make this scene different that the thousands of other scenes exactly like it? This was answered in "Patriot Games" by giving the cops (and the audience) a little something extra. A neat device that amazed the audience. The police take a fiber optic strand and slide it under the door of the bad guy's flat. They twist the strand around until they have thoroughly reconned the room. They know where every bad guy is, if he's armed, and what he's armed with. Once they have all of this knowledge, they crash open the door.

A neat idea. Something extra which makes this scene in "Patriot Games" different than all of the others. I don't know if this idea originated with Tom Clancy or the screenwriters, but I'm sure its genesis was in news reports about Doctors using fiber optic strands to recon the interior of the human body without major surgery. To transplant a device used in medicine to police work is genius at work.

Another neat idea popped up in Alan Sharp's "Rob Roy". Rob Roy has been captured by the army, under the command of his nemesis Archie. Hands tied, he is tethered to the back of a horse by about fifty feet of rope. No way to escape. He can only run fifty feet, before he reaches the end of his rope.

We have seen "escape from the badguys" scenes in a million films, but Alan Sharp treats us to something extra.

When the Army stops at a bridge over a raging river, and Archie dismounts, Rob Roy quickly runs up to him, twists the tether line around his neck, then jumps off the bridge. The rope strangles Archie (forcing the army to rescue him) and breaks Rob Roy's fall into the river (dangling him a few feet from the surface). The only way the Army can save Archie from strangulation is to cut the rope... and free Rob Roy!

Of all the possible ways for Rob Roy to escape, this method gives us the most for our money. It was such a neat idea, that the audience I saw it with cheered in amazement. Even a jaded professional screenwriter such as myself found myself cheering, and wishing that I had come up with that idea for one of my scripts.

In Scott Rosenberg's "Things To Do In Denver When You're Dead", that little something extra is the bizarre slang the gangsters use. Instead of "Goodbye", they say "Boat Drinks". An old timer translates this for us: While in prison, convicts dream of drinking cocktails on a yacht when they get out. Hence "Boat Drinks", which is a variation on "Have a nice day". Weird slang peppers this script, from "Buckwheats" to "Give it a name", giving the audience a little something extra.

There was a TV episode, I think from "Banacek", where a ton of gold bullion is stolen from vault overnight. But how was it removed? Too heavy to lift, too bulky to get past the posted guards. Of all the various methods available, the screenwriter chose the one with something extra. The gold bricks were stacked against the back wall of the vault and painted brick red. They had never been removed from the vault, just disguised to look like the vault's back wall.

One of the best ways to separate your script from the thundering heard is to fill it with neat ideas, give every scene something extra.

Go over your script scene by scene, and try to infuse each with something extra, either a neat device or a neat method. Whichever, it should be something we haven't seen before. Something which will have the audience talking about it long after the final credits have rolled.

BONUS TECHNIQUE!

"Match Cuts"

Match Cuts link scenes together using images or sounds (including dialogue). They find an element from the end of one scene and link it to an element from the beginning of the next scene. Like a hook-and-eye fastener in clothing. This creates an end for one scene which thrusts us into the next scene. Since it's important to start a scene as late as possible, a match cut allows you to begin with action in progress without confusing the audience.

The most common Match Cut is verbal to visual. You've seen it in a million movies. John asks Tom where he's going. "Las Vegas." If Tom is playing poker at a casino in the next shot, no one's going to ask: Where is he? How did he get there? They KNOW he's in Las Vegas.

There's a great example of Visual to Visual in "Blood Simple":

                    MARTY (vo)
          Listen asshole, it's Marty. I just got back
          from Corpus Christi and there's a lot of
          money missing from the safe. I told you to
          keep an eye on your asshole friend....

Maurice's index finger presses down on the answering machine's "off" button.

EXT.   RAY'S DRIVEWAY - DAY

Ray's index finger presses down on the back seat, and comes away covered with Marty's blood.

For some other examples watch "Point Blank", "Blood Simple", "Exorcist 2", "Psycho 3", "Petulia", "Don't Look Now", and "The Man Who Fell To Earth".

MOVING PICTURES

If a picture is worth a thousand words, and screenplays are supposed to be visual, then why do many readers and development executives skip over the descriptions? Poor reading skills and sub-standard IQs among studio personnel can only account for half of the problem, which means the other half is ours.

Many of us spend no time at all on images and visuals... making our scripts nothing more than stage plays with lots of set changes. Describing a house or a salt shaker in your script is not a visual.

A good visual creates an image which sticks with the viewer long after the house lights are up. It haunts us. Creating an emotional experience without words. Touching us on a subconscious level to give us an experience stronger than the image itself.

In mystery writer Michael Connelly's fine novel "The Concrete Blonde", a prostitute's body is thrown into a vat of wet concrete. When the murder is discovered many years later, the body has decomposed... except for the silicon modified breasts which are in perfect condition. This image of the wasted body with unnaturally perfect breasts is haunting. It gives us a glimpse of the victim, who put physical attraction above all else.

The image is filled with irony and tragedy, infused

with emotion. Years after reading the novel, this image comes back to me with perfect clarity.

That's good writing.

Another memorable image comes from Sidney J. Furie and Rick Natkin's under rated Viet Nam War film "The Boys In Company C". Stan Shaw plays a loner: A soldier who believes that depending on the other screwups in his platoon will get him killed.

While patrolling a rice paddy, Shaw steps on a mine. The moment he takes his foot off the mine, it will blow up, killing all of those around him. "Do not go near that man, leave him alone. He is a dead man." All of the other members of the platoon reluctantly move away, leaving Shaw standing alone in the middle of the rice paddy... Waiting to die.

The lone-man image was also used to great effect in "High Noon", where Gary Cooper steps onto the street, and the camera pulls back to show him alone. The streets deserted. The view of him from high overhead, seeming small and powerless, has haunted viewers since the film's initial release.

Scarlett O'Hara is a lone woman in "Gone With The Wind", crossing through an ocean of Confederate dead and wounded in the freight yards of Atlanta, looking for the doctor. As she passes the wounded, they reach out for her, but she ignores them. Batting away hands when they grab her. Again, the camera pulls high overhead... Exposing the Confederate flag, tattered, waving in the cannon smoke.

Some other images which linger long after the closing credits:

When Godfrey Tearle lifts his hand to expose a

missing little finger, and we know he's the villain in "The 39 Steps".

Paul Newman and Robert Redford taking that jump into the river in "Butch Cassidy And The Sundance Kid".

Jimmy Stewart looking from window to window in the darkness after hearing a scream in "Rear Window".

The rooftop dance in front of the giant Coca-Cola sign in "Strictly Ballroom".

Another great dance scene can be found in the movie "Witness".

Michael Caine forces a rusty nail into his palm to stop from being brainwashed in "The Ipcress File".

The bicycles flying across the sky in "E.T."

The rotting apple from "Robin And Marian".

Donald Sutherland, body pierced by a half dozen pitchforks, tries to escape an angry mob in "1900".

The drop of water turning the photograph red, which seems to predict the drowning of the protagonist's five year old daughter in "Don't Look Now" (and predict the protagonist's death, as well).

The cross cut sequence with Lee Marvin marching down an airport hallway to meet... His wife, whose heart pounds in rhythm with Marvin's shoes, from "Point Blank".

The short film "The Red Balloon", which is a series of amazing images, topped off by the shot of the balloon flying high above the city.

The great flashback from "Once Upon A Time In The West" where we learn the significance of Charles Bronson's harmonica.

Any Busby Berkeley dance number, especially the wacky and opulant ones from "42nd Street".

The frightening torture scene where a young and sexy Cloris Leachman is stripped naked by the villains... and then they grab a pair of pliers, from "Kiss Me Deadly".

"Vertigo" (which is mostly silent). Especially the scene where Jimmy Stewart has to climb the staircase to the belltower, and the floor seems to fall away from him.

Giant crosses created strong visual moments in Sam Fuller's "The Big Red One" and Dean Reisner's "Dirty Harry".

The hat blowing away in the Coen Brother's "Miller's Crossing".

A moth plastered against a window by falling rain in William Goldman's "Marathon Man".

The windmill in "Foreign Correspondent", with it's massive sails which catch the breeze one way, then move in the opposite direction.

HITCHCOCK

The sequence in "North By Northwest" where Cary Grant throws a matchbook with a warning written in it down to Eva Marie Saint, but it MISSES and hits the floor. Villain Martin Landau spots the match book and picks it up. Will he open it and discover the warning? Tension. Suspense. Finally Landau sets the matchbook in the ashtray, and the audience breathes again.

In fact, I could fill several pages with strong images and sequences from Hitchcock films. From Beaky being pushed off the cliff in "Suspicion" to the cigarette lighter just out of reach in the storm drain from "Strangers On A Train".

Though Hitchcock as a director deserves some credit for putting these images on film, it should be noted that they came directly from the pages of the screenplays. From "North By Northwest":

EXT. SECLUDED ROAD - A FEW MINUTES LATER

A lovely wooded glen securely hidden from the main
road that cuts through the Black Hills. The Mt.
Rushmore Monument can be seen in the distance
through the trees.
Thornhill and Eve regard each other uncertainly
as she starts moving toward him.

In a way, they are meeting for the first time.

After all that Eve has done to Thornhill, and he
has said to her, neither can be certain of the
others' true feelings.
It is a time for uneasiness, caution, and tenta-
tive probing. Eventually giving way to what has
always been apparent: the fact that they do like
each other more than somewhat.

A moment of silence. They move closer.

This is a very strong moment from the film, a
purely visual moment, and it began as words on a page
written by Ernest Lehman.

In William Goldman's "Adventures In The Screen
Trade", he quotes Rosalind Russell as saying, "Do you
know what makes a movie work? Moments. Give the
audience half a dozen moments that they can remember,
and they'll leave the theater happy." These moments,
whether they be single images or sequences of images,
are one of the most important elements of your screenplay... And one of the most ignored by screenwriters.
Far too many screenwriters believe that the visual
part of the film belongs to the director. But the director
can only interpret what's on the page. If your script
doesn't contain strong visual images which create an

emotional response in the audience, the best a director can do is to add a peripheral, unrelated image, which doesn't come from the story or characters. Hollow images which will not emotionally move the audience. Film is a collaborative medium, but that collaboration begins with our scripts.

If we have not written strong, emotionally charged images in our screenplays, it's doubtful that those "moments" necessary for a happy audience will end up in the film. And our films will ultimately fail.

The success of your action screenplay hinges not only on plotting, characterization, and dialogue; but on your ability to create hard images which haunt the audience long after the house lights have removed the shadows from the screen.

Visual "moments" which touch a chord with the viewer. A half dozen of those moments, and you've got yourself a movie... which will move the audience.

THE HAMLET MOMENT

I recently read a script by a new writer which was a real page turner. Non stop action, with the protagonist narrowly escaping one dangerous situation, only to find himself in a worse predicament. Real out of the fry pan into the fire stuff. Sounds exciting, right?

Well, the script was actually rather dull. It took me another read through to find the problem. The lead character seemed sketchy. He spent so much time running, we never had a chance to really know him. There was never a scene where he stopped to contemplate his fate. To let us in on his fears and anxieties.

I'm sure some of you are asking: What do you propose? Stopping the action for a moment of introspection? Some sort of speech like the soliloquy from "Hamlet"?

Yes. That's EXACTLY what I am proposing. "Hamlet" is an exciting tale of murder, mystery, and revenge. Filled with sword fights and intrigue. Yet the action stops about halfway through the script so that Hamlet can examine his mortality and his soul. He tells us his fears, and lets us in on the darkest of secrets which even his close friend Horatio knows nothing of. The audience becomes his confidant. His closest friend.

Wait a moment, you say. We're talking about an action script, here, not a drama! So let us look at "Die

Hard" by Jeb Stuart and Steven E. DeSouza, based on the novel by Roderick Thorp. Certainly not some stuffy drama... Yet about two thirds through the script (page 94), John McClane manages a very dramatic soliloquy about his mortality, and the mistakes he made in his marriage. A dramatic confession of past sins. He gives Officer Powell a message for his wife, in the event of his death.

This is the most powerful scene in the movie. The "Hamlet Moment" for the John McClane character. I should mention that this scene is not an actual soliloquy, not a speech. The screenwriters present it in the form of dialogue between McClane and Officer Powell. But the confessional nature of the scene gives almost all of the dialogue to McClane, with Powell adding comments and questions along the way.

In our modern world, the idea of an actual soliloquy, with a character talking to himself, seems rather silly. Best to present the scene as dramatic dialogue.

Officer Powell manages a Hamlet Moment of his own a few pages earlier (page 88) where he tells about accidentally killing and eleven year old kid, and his current fears and self doubts about his future as a policeman. Another juicy, dramatic scene. The kind every actor wants to play.

Scenes such as these serve two important purposes in your script. They allow the audience in on your protagonist's inner conflicts; making the reader more than just a casual acquaintance, but a close friend. And they give an actor a chance to act.

Remember: Actors want to act. Sylvester Stallone has taken a cut in pay to play a hearing impaired detective, forced to deal with his disabilities in the upcoming film "Copland". Bruce Willis is no stranger to drama, signing on to small roles for reduced pay in order to play dramatic characters in "Nobody's Fool" and several other films. Willis may make $20 million (or more) to run, jump, and shoot guns; but he became an actor to act. When he reads a script, he's looking for those dramatic scenes which will display his acting talents.

In order to attract actors to your work, to sign them to the project, there should be scenes where they are allowed to use whatever acting gifts they may have. This is what they will be looking for when they read the script. One rather famous actor is known to highlight "acting" passages and write "NAR" on lines where there is no acting required. After so marking the script, he gives it a final flip through... if there are too many passages with NAR written on them, he doesn't take the role.

Part of our job as screenwriters is to provide actors with a showcase for their talents. A few, well placed, big dramatic scenes serve not only the actor, but the audience and the story. Remember: Conflict is the basis of story, and drama is the natural growth of conflict.

In "Adventures In The Screen Trade", William Goldman says: "You must give the star everything." That includes at least one scene where the audience says to themselves: "Wow, that Sylvester Stallone really knows how to ACT!"

A Hamlet Moment where our characters are allowed to reveal themselves, to take the audience into their confidence. Even the fastest paced action script requires the audience to know and understand the protagonist in order to be effective.

Fully developed characters make us care. Look over your current script. Do you have at least one solid

119

dramatic scene where your protagonist reveals him/her-self? Have your provided the star with a role he/she can really sink her teeth into?

Writers like to tell stories, actors like to act.
Our common ground is a good dramatic scene.
A few good dramatic scenes will help attract actors to your script, which helps attract producers as well.

PERSONAL INJURIES

POP QUIZ. Which hurts more: hitting your elbow on a door frame or getting blasted by a laser?

The obvious answer is the laser blast, but it isn't the correct answer. If I were to show you a film clip where a man hit his elbow on a door frame, you'd go "ouch". You'd understand the pain and empathize with the man. But if I showed you a "Star Trek" clip where a laser dissolves a man, it wouldn't effect you. You've never been hit by a laser blast, you have no idea what it feels like.

We all know about the evils of abstracts. Mystery novelist and TV writer Joe Gores says in the Mystery Writer's Handbook, "Don't indulge in 'soft' writing. A street, means any street. A car, means any car. I want to see a specific street, a specific car. Hard detail is what makes a story believable."

You probably take special care when deciding whether your protagonist drives a sports car or a family sedan, if he wears tennis shoes or spats; but even specifics can be abstracts if the audience hasn't experienced them personally. Which takes us back to that laser gun. Even if you actually know how lasers work, create a brand name and specifications, fill in all the knobs and do-dads; the audience still won't feel the pain along with your laser blastee.

121

George Lucas figured out a way to by-pass this problem by creating 'light sabers', which are basically laser blades. They cut. We all know what it is like to get cut, don't we?

VIOLENCE IS AS VIOLENCE DOES

Using violence in your script is meaningless unless your audience can feel it. Remember: Film is communication. Your script must be designed to communicate with the audience (through the medium of the camera and the actors). The difference between effective violence and gratuitous violence is: Gratuitous violence isn't felt by the audience. It's just exploitation. Spurting blood and exploding heads. Who among us have had our heads explode? (If this HAS happened to you, please don't write me... I'd rather not know). So violence must be personalized.

Here are three examples of action scenes which work because the audience understands the results of the violence:

Steven deSouza and Jeb Stuart's "Die Hard" contains one of the most painful moments on film. John McClane is our barefoot hero, taking on a team of ruthless terrorists. Hans and Karl have cornered McClane in the Computer Room, and the three are involved in a shoot out.

```
HANS

looks at the glass all around him, gets and idea.
He SHOUTS to Karl:

                    HANS
          The glass! Shoot the glass!
```

And, saying this, he demonstrates.
Karl follows suit.

McCLANE

As glass flies everywhere, McClane sees one op-
tion and takes it. BLASTING a burst to keep their
heads down, he WHIRLS, JUMPS on top of a long
counter and RUNS ACROSS THE ROOM. Their BULLETS
follow him, six inches behind his moving form.

McClane reaches the end of the counter, DIVES to
the floor:

HIS FOOT

goes right down on a jagged SHARD. He groans,
keeps going.

STAIRWELL DOOR

He's out, gone, safe.

INT. BATHROOM - NIGHT

McClane all but crawls inside. His dragging foot
leaving a trail of blood on the linoleum. Wincing
in pain, McClane washes his foot in a sink basin.
He washes a deep cut, but the pain doesn't relent.

When I was a kid, I was walking barefoot in my
back yard and stepped on a nail. It went right through
my foot.

I'll bet, in your life, you once stepped on broken
glass while barefoot. It hurts. We know it hurts. When
John McClane drags himself into the bathroom, we know
EXACTLY how he feels. The pain is real for us, more
real than a shotgun blast.

My second example is from the classic Dean Riesner scripted "Play Misty For Me". Clint Eastwood is having a major ex-girlfriend problem: She is trying to kill him. With a knife. A very sharp knife. Do you know what 'defense wounds' are?

She attacks Clint with the knife, stabbing out at his face. Not wanting to get stabbed in the face, he catches the knife in his hand. Ouch! There's a close up shot of the blade slicing his fingers as he tries to hang onto it. Double ouch! Then she pulls the blade back, out of his hand, practically severing his fingers. Triple ouch!

How many of us have been chopping an onion and cut ourselves? Probably everyone. Again, we know EXACTLY how being cut with a knife feels. When it happens on screen, part of the audience's brain flashes back to the time THEY were cut, and they instantly feel the pain.

My last example is from a dark comedy film called "Swimming With Sharks" about a Personal Assistant who holds his mean spirited Boss hostage and metes out a strange revenge for on the job abuse. I've seen this film four times, and every time the audience jumps at one painful scene. Even though I know the scene is coming, it still affects me:

The Personal Assistant takes a crisp, clean, new piece of paper and slashes his Boss's face with paper cuts. Ouch! He also cuts his Boss's tongue with a sharp envelope flap. Ouch!

This scene was worse for me than "Play Misty For Me". I work with paper and envelopes EVERY DAY. Paper cuts hurt worse than anything else on earth (including that nail in the foot). And a paper cut on your tongue? I've had one before. The pain stays for weeks! If you haven't seen "Swimming With Sharks", it's well worth a rent. Oh, and did I mention the Boss is a film producer?

The key to writing an effective action sequence is to make sure the violence is something the audience understands, and can empathize with. As B-Movie Maven Fred Olen Ray once asked me: "If a man is shot by a laser and falls down, is the laser on stun or kill? Is he hurt or dead?" We don't know, because we've never been shot by a laser.

PAIN IS IN THE DETAILS

Personalizing action/violence/pain means showing us the DETAILS. Details which we understand. Say you have a plane crash survivor forced to search for help in a rocky terrain. He has been walking all day, and stops to take off his dress shoes. When he takes off his socks, we see the blisters on his feet. Big, painful blisters. Some have broken open, and when the air touches the nerve endings, our Survivor gasps in pain. Anyone who has ever had new dress shoes knows how this feels. Because this is drama, we have MAGNIFIED the injury and the pain. Taken it up a couple of notches.

Steven deSouza's "Commando" ends with an epic battle in the furnace room of a mansion. At one point, John Matrix's face is pressed against the furnace door. Sizzle! We know how that feels, from the time we lifted the pan without a pot holder. DeSouza has magnified the pain by making the furnace door red hot, and subject of the burn our hero's face. You know that's gotta hurt! When you are writing a fight scene, think of the detail. The personal injury which will make your audience gasp in identification. I like to have villains break my hero's fingers, either by crushing them or bending them backwards. We know that hurts.

Did you know that a pistol barrel gets hot after firing? Hot enough to burn? When I have two characters struggling with a gun which keeps discharging, I like to add in the burn factor. Grab the barrel... sizzle... ouch! We may not have burned our hands on a gun barrel, but we've burned our hands on SOMETHING. We know exactly how it feels.

We know how it feels to have someone step on our foot really hard, to get something in our eye, to get a pavement scrape, etc. These are the kinds of things to use in your action scenes to make them effective.

WHEN YOU WANT TO HURT THE WORLD

Your villain has spent his entire life hurting people one by one, and now he's ready to move on to world destruction and/or domination. He wants to blow up Cleveland or wipe out his enemies' family lines. How do you make such massive destruction personal? There are two ways to make big action effective on screen.

ONE: Make sure your protagonist has a stake in the outcome, and make sure the audience's identification with your protagonist is VERY strong.

A good example is Donald Stewart and W. Peter Iliff's "Patriot Games". We are introduced to family man Harrison Ford, his wife and daughter. We learn to care about them as a family. When Ford steps in to thwart a terrorist bombing, not only do the terrorist come after him, they come after his family as well. Ford must stop the Terrorists, because he and his family are directly threatened. If your villain is killing a bunch of people you don't know, or don't care about, it is meaningless violence. Giving a spear-carrier a scene where he is kind to small animals before he is killed just doesn't cut it.

Audiences see it coming from a mile away. Is there anyone in the world who saw "Top Gun" and didn't KNOW Goose was about to die after they suddenly introduce his wife and family halfway through the film?

TWO: Have the Villain's Plan threaten the audience. We are sitting in the theater, minding our own business, when the Villain threatens to unleash a virus which will spread like wildfire. We see a map of the United States, and Donald Sutherland shows us how far the virus will spread in 24 hours... 48 hours... 96 hours (entire map is covered).

Now the audience is affected by the villain's plan. If the hero doesn't stop him WE will die. This method works best in films like "Fail Safe" and "War Games", where a nuclear incident will start a nuclear war which will probably destroy the world. The audience itself is threatened by the villain's actions. We will become the victims.

In my script "Crash Dive!", a group of terrorists have hijacked a 688 Attack Class nuclear submarine, and are threatening to nuke New York. Because I realized that might sound like a good idea to some audience members, I added the threat of firing at some random "small town" targets as well. Like the very city where the movie theater you're watching "Crash Dive!" is located in. Now you, the viewer, have a stake in the outcome.

The ultimate audience threat was in the William Castle film "The Tingler". At the end of the film, the Tingler escapes into a movie theater... the one YOU'RE sitting in! Vincent Price looks RIGHT AT YOU and warns you "It's under your seat". Theaters were wired with buzzers under some of the seats to reproduce the feeling of the Tingler's attack. I'm sure a few people jumped.

THIS WON'T HURT A BIT!

The one thing you don't want to do when creating violence in an action scene is to make it ineffective and painless. If the audience doesn't feel anything when a character is killed or injured, that's akin to pornography. It's violence desensitized.

In Shane Black's "The Last BoyScout", one of our heroes gets a knife stuck RIGHT THROUGH HIS HAND. He is pegged to a desk. He pulls the knife out, wraps a handkerchief around the wound, and is as good as new. This very violent act was without pain, without feeling... desensitized.

In Shane Black's "The Long Kiss Goodnight", Henessey gets beat up, shot a dozen times, blown out of an exploding building, and manages to walk away unharmed. None of the violence in this script has any effect on anyone. Getting blown out of a building doesn't matter to Henessey, so why should it matter to the audience? Getting shot doesn't matter. Getting hit doesn't matter. When the bad guys kidnap Charly's daughter... it just doesn't matter to us. If they shoot her, she'll just get up and walk away, right? Wrong. In real life pain hurts. Our job as screenwriters is to make an emotional connection with our audience. To INVOLVE them. To allow them to feel our characters' pain, and our characters' joys. To do that, we must personalize our stories and our action scenes and make the audience an active participant in our script.

When you get ready to write the next draft of your action script, just remember: This time, it's PERSONAL.

THREE ACT ACTION

William Goldman says the most important thing in screenwriting is STRUCTURE. Even "soft stories" like romances require good structure. So it shouldn't be any surprise that hard, plot-driven action stories are dependent upon structure. Without it, you're D.O.A. (the awful 1988 version). If you're looking for a good example of structure, study any successful action film.

"Witness" has been used as an example of three act structure by a half dozen script gurus, and for good reason. It follows the basic three acts of action films. What are these three acts? Lets look at another popular recipe...

ACT ONE: Every action film begins with the SET UP. Whether it's "Witness", "Code Of Silence", "Point Blank", or "The Set Up" (1949). You've got 25-30 pages to introduce your lead character and fully develop him. Once Act 1 is over, your lead will be involved in escalating conflict, and there won't be time to plant inner conflict, explain motivation, or add character information. Everything the audience needs to know about your lead will be expressed in the Set Up.

In the Set Up you should also introduce your villain. If, for some reason, you can't SHOW your actual villain this early in the script, introduce him by proxy through a

HENCHMAN. The Henchman symbolizes the villain, and does his bidding.

By the end of Act 1, we should have some understanding of the VILLAIN'S PLAN. In "Lethal Weapon", the Villain and his Henchman are introduced in the first act, and their plan (to smuggle guns) is exposed. You may want to hold back all of the details of the Villain's Plan to use as a TWIST later, but we should get a clue what they're up to in Act 1.

The sooner you introduce your conflict, the better. This doesn't necessarily mean starting with an action sequence, though.

In my script "Shooter On The Side" the hero has a gun drawn on him on page one when he enters a closed bar and is mistaken for a burglar. There is a moment of tension, then the hero explains that he's only there to apply for a job. The gun is lowered, but the potential for violence between these two men remains. One will eventually rob the bar, the other will be accused of the crime and have to prove his innocence. By the end of the script, the two men will be in the same position, but both will be armed this time.

On page ONE I've set up the conflict which plays out through the rest of the script.

A bad script will use a bogus action sequence to start the film. A scene which has nothing to do with the hero or villain. The opening of "The Last BoyScout" has nothing to do with the rest of the film, except that it takes place on a football field. If Bruce Willis had been a cop investigating the football player's suicide, the opening scene would be organic. Make sure when you introduce action, it involves the Hero or the Villain.

The SET UP ends with the Hero and Villain on a collision course. Some major action will occur which will completely involve the hero in stopping the villain. In "The Big Heat" (1953) the villain plants a bomb in the Hero's car. The hero's wife and daughter borrow the car and BOOOOOOM! End Act 1.

ACT TWO: The hero on the run. Sometimes he's physically on the run, like in "The Fugitive" and "Witness"; other times he's emotionally and psychologically on the run. The hero will confront the villain, but back away instead of attack. In "Witness" John Book investigates by phone while he hides out with the Amish. In "The Big Heat" the cop tries to capture the villain through legal means.

In Act 2 the hero will avoid inner and outer conflicts, hoping that the problems will solve themselves. But the more he runs from his problems, the bigger they become. Until the end of Act 2, when a MAJOR action sequence will threaten the hero's life. In "Code Of Silence" the badguys beat the crap out of Chuck Norris and will butcher the female lead at sunrise if Norris doesn't hand over a rival mobster to the villain. By the end of Act 2, the hero will reach his "Popeye Point", where "he's had alls he can stands and he can't stands no more". He can't run anymore, so he must turn and fight. He solves his inner conflict, and gets ready to solve his outer conflict... with a machine gun!

ACT THREE: Is the final confrontation. It usually begins with a "gun worship" scene, where the hero gears up to do battle. In "Commando", "Code Of Silence", "The Wild Bunch", "Yakuza", and almost every action film made, there is a scene at the beginning of Act

3 where the hero straps on his guns, puts on his war-paint, and gets ready to kill badguys.

From that point on, Act 3 in an action film should be non-stop action. Wall to wall action. A car chase leads to a shoot out leads to a fist fight leads to another chase leads to a shoot out. In Act 2, the villain chases the hero. In Act 3, the hero chases the villain. Watch the last 30 minutes of "Lethal Weapon", it's a ROLLER COASTER of action scenes from the escape until the final shoot out.

Act 3 of "Code Of Silence" is a huge shoot out in a warehouse, with Chuck Norris against an army of bad guys. The warehouse shootout runs about 25 minutes, and is filled with twists, turns, and reversals. Act 3 of any James Bond movie usually has Bond and a small group of commandos raiding the villain's secret stronghold. There is a huge gun battle, ending with the villain's escape. Bond battles the lead henchman (who's usually a musclemen), then catches the villain moments before he can escape. Bond and the villain face off for a "High Noon" style confrontation. The villain and Bond have usually tangled twice before: In Act 1, where they played golf, and in Act 2, where the villain completely STOMPED Bond and left him for dead. Can Bond possibly win the rematch in Act 3? Well, he has so far in 17 films.

A great example of act 3 action can be found in "Shaft's Big Score!" (1972). The last 30 minutes of the film is wall-to-wall action with only ONE line of dia-logue: "He's got a boat!". Act 3 begins with the funeral of a black gangster, which turns into a huge machine gun fight when the Mafia shows up. The machine gun fight evolves into a car chase, as Shaft tries to catch the Mafia

hit men. Then the tables are turned on Shaft, as a helicopter attacks his car. There is a car/helicopter chase,
which ends when Shaft's car crashes on a pier. Shaft
grabs a boat, and the chase is back on. The boat/heli-
copter chase is pretty hairy: Shaft speeds under some
low bridges to shake off the chopper. Finally Shaft runs
the boat aground, where it EXPLODES! Now Shaft is
being chased on the pier by the helicopter. He plays
hide and go seek on the pier with the helicopter, and
some Mafia guys on foot. Then Shaft hides in a dark
warehouse. BUT THE HELICOPTER FLIES INTO THE
WAREHOUSE!

There's a neat INDOOR helicopter chase, then
Shaft runs up some catwalks. The Helicopter chases Shaft
along the catwalks, and they exchange gunfire. That's
when the Mafia foot soldiers find him. There's a fight
and shoot out on the catwalks. Shaft kills the foot soldiers, then tries to escape the helicopter. But he's trapped!
Shaft and the helicopter exchange gunfire, until Shaft
hits the gas tank. BLAAAM!! The helicopter explodes
into a million pieces... The cops arrive (too late to do
anything, as usual) and silently congratulate Shaft.

The End.

Thirty SOLID minutes of action with only one
line of dialogue! That's what an Act 3 should be like!

BUDDY COP FILMS

Have two variations on the three act structure.

In one version ("48 Hours", "They Live", "Rush
Hour"), the partners absolutely hate each other, trading
insults and punches until the middle of Act 2. That's
when they finally square off to fight. They beat the crap
out of each other and gain insight and respect with every
punch (huh?). By the end of the fight, they've learned

to tolerate each other, and begin working together to solve the crime.

The other variation ("Lethal Weapon") has the "screw up" partner saving the "mainstream" partner's life at the beginning of Act 2. The screw up continues to provide help, which the mainstream partner grudgingly accepts. At the end of Act 2, the action affects the mainstream partner personally, and he has no one to turn to for help but the screw up partner. So they team up 100% to battle the villains.

Name a buddy cop film, and it will fit into one of those two models. Both use the same Act 1 and Act 3, but have different ways of solving the partner conflicts in Act 2.

So remember the three basic acts of Action Films:
Act 1: The Set Up.
Act 2: Hero On The Run.
Act 3: Hero Turns And Fights.
And keep the action moving. Like a FREIGHT TRAIN. Relentlessly speeding towards the conclusion, where the hero and villain face off for their High Noon confrontation.

BANG!
BANG!
BANG!
The Villain is killed, and the Hero can walk off into the sunset with the Love Interest.

LOVE INTERESTS

Throughout this book, I've tried to keep the sex of the hero neutral. Your hero might be a female private eye (like Sue Grafton's Kinsey Mallone) or a female version of Paul Kersey from "Death Wish" (like Abel Ferrara's "Ms.45" or my unproduced script "Rogan's Wife"). But the fact is, 95% of all action leads are men; which means the love interest is probably going to be female (unless you're doing a film version of Joseph Hansen's tough private eye Dave Brandstetter). So feminists, bare with me, as I explain the role of love interests in the average action script.

Burned out cops, Private Eyes, and CIA Agents seldom have girlfriends or wives. They usually fall for a dame involved in their case. More often than not, it's the WRONG dame. A no good tart who leads our hero to his doom. In the end, our hero either gives her a rap on the mouth or a slug from a 45 automatic. But he always remembers her. Have we exorcised that cliche? Good. Now let's get real.

Not all heros need love interests. Dirty Harry doesn't have much time for romance in most of his films. Ah-nuld spends more time with his machine guns than with women (when he does get a love interest, it's usually a wife... like in "True Lies" and "Total Recall"). Nick Cage's love interest in "Con Air" is the wife he's trying to get home to... he spends 99% of the film with a bunch of grimy convicts! I'm still trying to figure out why Julia Roberts kissed the creepy psycho stalker played by Mel Gibson in "Conspiracy Theory". I believed Mel loving her, I just couldn't buy Julia loving him back. He's a weirdo!

Don't try to force a love interest into your film, just to add gratuitous nudity, romance, or a sex scene.

In my techno-thriller film "Steel Sharks", the hero is a captured Navy SEAL trying to escape. No time for romance! The film has helicopters, Gary Busey in a submarine, F-14 fighter planes, and Billy Dee Williams as the Admiral of an aircraft carrier in the Persian Gulf. The only woman in the entire film is Williams' tough, competent attache, Ms. Hickey. Love interest? Nope. The hero doesn't even meet Ms. Hickey! If your script doesn't need a love interest, don't feel like you are required to add one. If you think a love interest is a good idea, read on...

SUSPECTS

For a love interest to be integral to the plot, rather than something glued on to provide a little nudity, she's probably going to be a suspect. That doesn't mean she's a cliche femme fatale. But it does mean she will probably be related to the victim in some way.

In "The Big Sleep", Marlowe has a central love interest, Vivian Rutledge, and a secondary love interest, Vivian's sister Carmen. Either woman may have killed Sean Regan. Vivian is involved in an illegal scam with gambler Eddie Mars. Carmen poses for porno pictures, and may have killed the pornographer, A.G. Geiger. The Marlowe/Vivian relationship was an invention of the screenwriters, and is a textbook example of the suspect love interest. Neither one trusts the other, and much of their romantic bantering has an undercurrent of third degree questioning. As the relationship progresses, Marlowe finally has it out with Vivian. In a speeding car, he pulls the truth from her... and discovers that she's NOT the murderer. From that point on, they band together to catch the killer.

If the love interest is a suspect, she can't be the primary suspect without moving into "Noir/Erotic Thriller" territory, like "Basic Instinct" or my cable film "Hard Evidence". She can't be the secondary suspect, as they're usually the killer. So the love interest has to be a minor suspect; someone who might be the killer, but probably isn't. Just enough for suspicion, but not so much that the hero and love interest trade machine gun fire in the last reel.

I HAVE YOUR WIFE!

In Act 3, where it "gets personal", the love interest is frequently kidnaped by the villain. This ups the ante. But while she's kidnaped; don't have her sit there, have her DO something. Try to escape like Alyssa Milano did in Steven DeSouza's "Commando". Beat up a minor henchman. Create a weapon out of a pencil, a rubber band, and a ruler. You're writing an action script, so keep the action going strong. If the love interest is too much of a wimp, or if all she does is stand around and scream during the fight scenes, the audience is going to wonder why the hero wants to save her in the first place.
Both "Lethal Weapon" and "Face/Off" use a different kind of love: the girl kidnapped in these films is

the protagonist's daughter. When violent FBI Agent John Travolta realizes the terrorist villain he's pursuing has made this 'Take Your Daughter To Work Day', he is torn between protecting the daughter he has come to ignore and indiscriminate machine gunning in the villain's general direction. "Face/Off", like "Die Hard", is really a story which explores families in crisis against a background of things exploding real good. Both use their action plots to fuel the type of smaller, personal stories usually found in dramas. In a strange way, "Face/Off" is the action version of "Ordinary People"... both films are about how the death of a son affects a family.

The "kidnaped girl" has become such a hoary old cliche in action films, I would shy away from it if possible, or try to find a new angle. In "Lethal Weapon 2" the love interest is murdered by the villain at the beginning of Act 3... Making it very difficult for Riggs to walk off into the sunset with her. But giving him a hell of a good reason to kick badguy's butts.

DIVORCE COURT

Another type of love interest is the "dysfunctional relationship". In "48 Hours" Nick Nolte and the beautiful Annette O'Toole spend all of their scenes bickering. She doesn't understand his work. Since all they do is fight, Nolte becomes MORE involved in his work, and the relationship crumbles. Finally he solves his case, goes home, and makes up.

This same situation was used in the prequel to "Die Hard", 1968's "The Detective" (based on a great novel by Rod Thorp) starring Frank Sinatra in the part later played by Bruce Willis. In "The Detective" Sinatra and his wife, played by Lee Remick, are in a rocky marriage (she doesn't understand his work) which pushes him deeper into his case (a brutal murder in New York's Gay community) and ends up leading to their divorce... Setting the scene for their reconciliation 17 years later in "Die Hard". Using a dysfunctional relationship is a way to bring out the blind dedication of the hero on his quest to vanquish the villain.

SHE COMPLETES ME

The third type of love interest is rare in action films: Woman as redeemer. This is best illustrated in Nicholas Ray's "On Dangerous Ground" (1952).

Robert Ryan plays a brutal cop who beats up one too many suspects and is transferred to snow covered upstate New York... just in time to catch a killer. In this beautiful, pastoral setting, he blasts after the killer... a bull in a china shop. But softens when he falls in love with the suspect's blind sister played by Ida Lupino. Instead of railroading the suspect into the electric chair, the cop ends up going by the book. This is an interesting film, sort of a predecessor to "Witness", finally available on video.

EQUAL TIME

"Lethal Weapon 3" created the love interest for the today's action films. A female cop as rough and tough as Riggs. She can stomp bad guys, AND kiss good guys. Their scar comparison love scene is a classic... even though it's a rip off from "Jaws".

Rene Russo seems to be the tough gal of choice these days, playing a Secret Service Agent opposite Clint Eastwood in Jeff Maguire's brilliant "In The Line Of Fire"

139

and back beside Mel Gibson in "Lethal Weapon 4".

If at all possible, I'd suggest making your love interest a tough, competent woman who can take care of herself. Although the primary audience for action films is men, they usually bring a date. If your film can appeal to both sexes, you could have a hit on your hands.

IS NUDITY IS REQUIRED?

Because of the violence, action films are usually R rated. Producers figure, since they already have an R, why not throw in some nudity? It might help sell the film overseas. "Lethal Weapon 2" has a nude scene, "48 Hours" has a nude scene, and even "Die Hard" manages to throw in a couple of breasts during the office party which opens the film. Though action films seem to be moving out of R rated territory in favor of the teen audience who flock to PG-13 films, let's spend a couple of minutes covering nudity.

One cliche method of injecting nudity in your script is by having the cops go to a topless bar. I don't recommend it. Not only have we seen it a million times, but it makes the nudity part of the background action, and therefor unimportant. If it's unimportant, why is it even in the movie?

SEX AND VIOLENCE

Be careful when creating your nude scene. Remember that a rape scene is NOT a sex scene... it's a violence scene! Using a rape as your way to include nudity is not only in bad taste, it works against the very reason nudity is required in action films. It doesn't titillate, it repulses. For the same reason, you can't cross cut a sex scene and a violence scene. Many producers think that because nudity is exciting, and violence is exciting; combining both will be twice as exciting. Wrong! We are talking radically different kinds of excitement. Violence creates the excitement of fear. Nudity creates sexual excitement. Fear tends to cancel out sexual excitement. So cross cutting sex and violence is a great way to cancel out any excitement you might have had by using each emotion separately. In fact, the only way to combine sex and violence in your script is to give a naked woman a machine gun... And that image produces laughter rather than excitement. Check out "Jackie Brown" if you don't believe me.

NUDE ON A SUBMARINE

On my HBO World Premiere movie "Crash Dive!", the director insisted on a sex scene. It's a submarine warfare film, which takes place on a US 688 Class nuclear submarine.

"There are 110 men on the submarine, what kind of sex did you have in mind?" I asked.

In the script, the hero's love interest is Admiral Frederic Forrest's attache (played by beautiful Catherine Bell from "JAG"). They spent the entire film thousands of miles away from each other flirting by short burst radio. No chance for nudity there. The plot has a group of terrorists hijacking the sub on the high seas. One of the terrorists was a woman. "There's you sex scene!" the director said. After much arguing about why a terrorist would stop running and shooting long enough to indiscriminately bed down with some stranger, I wrote the scene. It's the silliest scene in the film.

Everyone who has seen the film mentions how out of place the sex scene is in this particular action plot.

Not every script needs a sex scene, and some (like "Crash Dive!") are much better off without them.

KISS KISS BANG BANG

The best way to incorporate nudity into your action script is through a romantic sex scene between your hero and the love interest. This scene also serves to show a gentle side of the hero, which may not be apparent in those scenes where he fires two machine guns into an army of villains.

Don't just have your hero and the love interest hop into bed, build the relationship through a progression of scenes. When it seems right for them to end up in bed together, give them one more flirt scene before they hit the sheets. This creates a romantic reversal and payoff, which will thrill the audience.

Movies like "Die Hard", "Con Air", "True Lies", "Face/Off", and my cable film "Hard Evidence" use wives as the love interest. In all five films the hero's relationship with his wife is in trouble (Inner Conflict), and through the action plot (Outer Conflict) comes to the realization that she is the love of his life. My friend calls these 'family values pictures' because they glorify the institutions of marriage and family. With Baby Boomers settled in to their married lives, I think we're going to see more films where the love interest is the hero's wife.

In scripts where the love interest is a suspect, there is often a post-sex scene where the sidekick finds a piece of evidence pointing to her as the killer. Now the hero must choose between relationships. The love interest, or the sidekick.

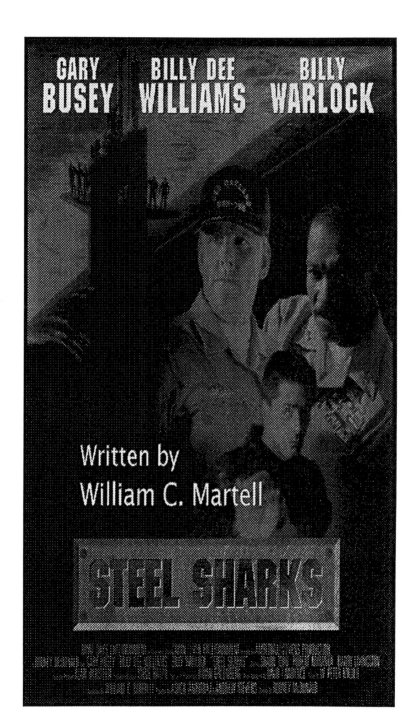

GARY BILLY DEE BILLY
BUSEY WILLIAMS WARLOCK

Written by

William C. Martell

STEEL SHARKS

SIDEKICKS

From Tonto to Dr. Watson to Hannibal Lecter (think about it) heroes have always had sidekicks to advise them and give them someone to chat with between shootouts. Since heroes are usually the strong silent type, sidekicks are often necessary to reveal clues and keep the dialogue peppy. Sidekicks are the brains to match the hero's brawn.

The Sidekick's main jobs are to help the hero, provide comic relief, and be murdered by the henchman at the end of Act 1 or the end of Act 2. In Shane Black's "The Last Action Hero" one of the best moments comes when the kid realizes that he's helping Arnold with his case and cracking jokes... This makes him the comic relief sidekick, which means he will be killed before the film is over.

When creating your sidekick, make sure he or she (I often use female sidekicks) have a special knowledge or talent which will aid the hero. The cliche is the computer nerd sidekick, who can hack into any system to find top secret information which will give the hero an edge or tell him what the badguys are really up to. I've seen enough hacker sidekicks to last a lifetime, so try to come up with something else.

In NBC's 1940s radio show "Candy Matson YU2-8209", female private eye Candy had a Gay sidekick named Rembrant who was an expert on antiques and fine art. Every week Candy would stumble into some action packed case which would involve art forgeries or antiques, so that Rembrant could supply the important clue which would crack the case. If a major network could have a gay antique expert as a sidekick in the 1940s, you can certainly do the same in a movie today.

THE CONTRAST KEY

Your sidekick character should be in contrast to your hero. If one's an introvert, the other should be an extrovert. The reason for this is for one to bring out the character in the other. If both are too much alike, we'll have trouble telling them apart, and they won't naturally bring out the character in each other. My pessimism comes to surface in the presence of someone who is overly optimistic. My neatness comes to surface in the presence of a slob. If everyone in the room is acting too serious, I can't help but come up with jokes. Use contrast between hero and sidekick to bring out the character in each.

The hero of my film "Night Hunter" (1995) is the last of the vampire hunters... A not-quite-human subspecies born and raised to kill blood suckers. He roars into town on his cycle, armed with his sawed off shotgun, killing tools, and an ancient book listing all the known vampire families. Cutter is a tortured man. A loner who lives by night, can't trust anyone, and kills for a living.

If there was ever a hero who needed a comedy relief sidekick, it's him. Because my theme was "belief", I needed to populate my script with skeptics, and I started with the sidekick. She's the ultimate skeptic, a reporter for the World Inquisitor tabloid who regularly covers alien abductions and Elvis sightings. I tried to infuse her dialogue with that Ben Hecht / "The Front Page" style sarcasm and machine gun fast delivery.

Even though much of her bantering was cut, Melanie Smith (who made out with Seinfeld at "Schindler's List") played the character to perfection. Her special skills are the Inquisitor's database of vampire stories, which provides clues to help Cutter plus evidence that vampires might exist to the Detective who wants to arrest Cutter as a serial killer. She also brings Cutter out of his shell... as she begins to believe in vampires, he begins to believe in trusting others again.

If there had been romance between them, she'd be "woman as redeemer".

HE AIN'T HEAVY, HE'S MY BUDDY

A variation on the sidekick is the buddy cop. There are four main types of buddy cops:

1) Old Cop partnered with Rookie Cop.
2) Good Cop partnered with Corrupt Cop.
3) Cop from one department partnered Cop from another department.
4) Sane Cop partnered with Crazy Cop.

In every buddy cop movie, one cop is always the hero and one is always the sidekick. Know which is which before you begin writing. If your hero ends up with more than one sidekick, you have a "Team Effort", which will be discussed in the next chapter. An important thing to remember is that buddy cops need not be cops. You can partner any two franchises to create something different. How about a defense lawyer and a private eye? (Perry Mason). A private eye and a samurai? ("The Yakuza"). Mad Max's sidekick in "The Road Warrior" was that crazy guy in the autogyro who did nothing but chatter and complain.

In my script "Recall", I partner a test driver for Road & Track Magazine with a tough female bodyguard to investigate a car which is "unsafe at any speed". The possibilities are limitless, so try to come up with something other than old cop/young cop or black cop/white cop. Be creative!

DYING IS EASY

No matter what his occupation, Sidekicks find it hard to get life insurance. The statistics show that most Sidekicks die at the end of Act 2, cradled in the hero's arms, uttering the last words: "Avenge me". The next scene usually shows the hero loading his guns and preparing for battle.

An alternative pops up from time to time, where the sidekick dies at the end of Act 1, pushing a reluctant hero into action. This was done in "Robo Cop 3", requiring the costume for spunky Nancy Allen's return in "Robo 4" to be made of metal.

Be careful when killing your sidekick on page 35! He or she must be a fully developed, likable character, before they get snuffed! Or else the audience just won't care whether the hero vows vengeance or not.

Usually the Villain just gives the order for the Sidekick's murder, it's up to the Henchman to do the bloody deed.

HENCHMEN

As the Sidekick is the brains to the Hero's brawn, the Henchman is the brawn to the Villain's brains. Villains sip cocktails and order the destruction of the world as we know it, Henchmen do the actual killing.

The perfect henchman is Odd Job from "Goldfinger":

1) He's PHYSICALLY POWERFUL, a guy about the size of Cleveland, Ohio. He towers over Bond, and is able to toss him around the room with little effort. When Bond slams a 2x4 into Odd Job's face in a fight, it breaks over the Henchman's head, and Odd Job smiles. Odd Job knows martial arts, too. One of the most important things to remember when creating your henchman: he has to be able to stomp the hero. When the audience sees the Henchman and the Hero fight, they have to be betting on the Henchman to win.

2) He has a SPECIAL WEAPON, that razor edged hat. All Henchmen have to have a special weapon, and the weirder the better. I don't mean you should make the Henchman an expert at killing people with ripe tomatoes; but if your choice is between a gun and a compound hunting bow... go with the bow and arrows. The audience should be able to identify the weapon with the

henchman. So when they see that hat sailing at Tilly Masterson, they KNOW that Odd Job can't be too far behind. That means only ONE special weapon per Henchman!

3) Odd Job is PHYSICALLY DIFFERENT. He's a mute (making him the ultimate strong silent type). He's also the only Korean in the entire film (even though he was played by a Japanese). The James Bond movies are a good place to learn about Henchmen, because every Bond film has a good Henchman. Even the silly ones like Jaws in "The Spy Who Loved Me" follow the pattern (metal dentures must be a pain at airport security stations).

4) Odd Job ENJOYS HIS WORK. He smiles after tossing Bond across the room. There's a touch of sadist in Henchmen, which makes the audience ill at ease. There is no way a hero can bribe a henchman to quit... Henchmen like to hurt people.

Henchmen are also impervious to pain.

I mentioned Odd Job smiling after being hit be a 2x4, but in "Lethal Weapon" Gary Busey's Henchman has a lighted cigarette ground out on his hand and smiles the entire time. This sequence is the introduction to Busey's character, and we know right away that Riggs is no match for him. As early as possible, give your henchman a display of strength so that we know how tough he is. In "Lethal Weapon", we eagerly wait for the scene pitting Busey and Gibson against each other, because we KNOW that Busey is the stronger of the two.

By the way, Busey also seems to enjoy his work, and has that freakish albino white hair, making him a perfect Henchman.

Henchmen have followed the above 4 rules since the beginning of time. Here's a description of henchman Eddie Prue from Raymond Chandler's 1942 novel "The High Window":

"A great long gallows of a man with a ravaged face and a haggard frozen right eye that had a clotted iris and the steady look of blindness. He was so tall that he had to stoop to put his hand on the back of the chair across from me."

After studying all of the Bond films for their use of Henchmen, you would be well served to read Chandler's thrillers (all available in paperback) for additional information. You'll not only enjoy the books, but come away with a few interesting plot and character ideas.

My best henchman is Mr. Deitrich from "Hard Evidence". I wanted to come up with a completely unpredictable character: he could be laughing one minute and killing you the next. His rapid mood swings make him like the sweating dynamite in "The Wages Of Fear", you never know when he's going to explode. Colin Cunningham played the role perfectly. When Gregory Harrison finally fights back, slamming him to the ground, Cunningham laughs as if this is the funniest thing that's ever happened to him. Harrison points his gun at him, trying to force information from him. This provokes more laughter... What Harrison doesn't know is that the henchman has backed into his fallen gun. Reversal!

Love Interests and Henchmen round out your cast of characters and keep your action plot working on more than one level, but what happens when the hero has more than one sidekick?

You end up with a TEAM EFFORT.

BONUS TECHNIQUE!

"Punchlines"

Punchlines work like punchlines in a joke. The fewest words possible to give the biggest impact, usually a twist. The idea is the find the BIGGEST way to end your scene, and use it. The operative word in Punchline is PUNCH. You want your scenes to end with a fist in the face... figuratively.

In my "Moondance" script, a group of film folks on ski vacation at the chalet of a violet eyed ex-Film Queen get snowed in. During the night, the Film Queen's dog is attacked by a werewolf. The group spends the next day boarding up the windows and doors of the chalet and hanging garlic. "That ought to keep it out," Pete says, hammering the last nail. John looks at the blocked windows and doors, "Or keep it in." BAM! On to the next scene.

The idea is to spring a shocker on your audience at the very end of the scene, then jump into the next scene before they have time to get over it.

The shocker can be anything from "I'm pregnant" to "I'm gay" to "I'm your father, Luke" to "I killed my first wife" (great scene ender in "Rebecca").

A little twist right before you cut to the next scene will keep those pages turning!

TEAM EFFORTS

Team efforts pop up more often in action movies than in any other genre. From "The Guns Of Navarone" to "Buckaroo Banzai" to "The Guns Of The Magnificent Seven" to "The Ronin", action heroes are frequently cheaper by the (Dirty) dozen. But Team Efforts are the most difficult type of action script to write; and for some unusual reason, the kind of script most likely to be written be a novice. It could be they idolize Tarantino, or think more characters equals less plot, or think with five leads each can be less fully developed. Wrong!

Whenever you have five of anything at the same time (babies, pets, girlfriends) it is at least five times more complicated. You not only have to squeeze more characterization into less screen time, you have to juggle all of these plots and subplots.

Am I trying to talk you out of writing a Team Effort script? Yes. But if you grew up reading Alastair MacLean, Don Westlake, and Doc Savage pulps; you're going to try to write one anyway, so we might as well learn how to do it right.

TAKE ME TO YOUR LEADER

Even the Dirty Dozen had a leader (Lee Marvin). Every team can be broken down into a Hero and his Sidekicks. There is no such thing as an ensemble action film. Give all of the guys in "Diner" a machine gun and set them against an army of terrorists, and you've got a disorganized mess.

Teams have leaders, and the leader is the hero. That means the leader is the character whose inner conflict grows into the outer conflict with the villain. In "The Wild Bunch", it's not Ernest Borgnine's character who used to be Robert Ryan's best friend, it's William Holden's character. The central conflict in "The Wild Bunch" is between Robert Ryan and William Holden (they get the flashbacks), the other characters are just along for the ride. Even William Holden's decision to go into town and rescue/avenge Angel is based upon his past relationship with Robert Ryan.

You have to know who the team leader is before you begin to plot your script. The team leader is the hero and has to take the hero's job: vanquishing the villain. No other team member is allowed to kill the villain. And the hero/villain relationship described in the Hero chapter of this book must be observed.

"Predator" begins as a team effort, but by the end it's Ah-nuld who camouflages himself to attack the creature, not Sonny Landham or Carl Weathers or Shane Black. Who ever you chose as Team Leader (Hero) will remain the hero until the end of the script.

In some war films, the hero isn't the actual team leader, but he IS the POV character, and ends up leading the team after the commander is killed. Sam Fuller's "Steel Helmet" is a good example of this. Gene Evans becomes the leader after half his division is wiped out... but the story was told from his point of view from the very beginning. Another Sam Fuller film, "Fixed Bayonets" (1951), takes a different tact. The story is told from the POV of the fourth in command, played by Richard Basehart. He is "just one of the team", okay at following orders but afraid to make decisions. Fuller builds suspense by having Basehart's three superiors killed one by one, forcing him to confront his fear of leadership.

True to the "hero on the run" Act 2, Basehart does everything in his power to make sure his superiors don't get killed... to the point of insane heroics! Realizing how close he came to getting killed just to avoid making decisions acts as the catalyst for his character's change. Finally he leads his team to victory.

THE DOC SAVAGE DELINEATION

Once you've got your leader (hero) it's time to fill out the rest of the team (sidekicks). The other members follow the guidelines for creating sidekicks in the previous chapter with one important addition. Sure, each member has to help the hero, and one of them might provide comic relief, and at least one of them will probably be killed by the henchman at the end of Act 1 or Act 2... But the important addition is: They all have to be different.

Remember the contrast between the hero an the sidekick? That contrast increases exponentially when you have five sidekicks, each contrasting with the hero, and each contrasting with each other.

Sounds difficult? It gets worse.

Each team member should have his or her own character arc. Each team member should have a special talent or knowledge. Each team member should have a special weapon. Each team member should speak differently, so that if you were to cover the character headings in dialogue, you could easily tell them apart just by speech patterns and pet words and phrases. Each team member must have a different look, so that you can tell them apart at a glance.

In the Doc Savage pulp novels about a team of adventurers who saved the world from a maniacal villain every month (mostly written by Lester Dent). Doc Savage, the "Man Of Bronze" was the team leader. Tall, muscular, good looking. Indiana Jones meets Ah-nuld with a little James Bond thrown in for good measure.

Doc's five man team of "associates":

Renny: The world's top engineer. Over six feet tall. An ex-boxer with massive ham-sized fists.

Johnny: Expert in geology and archaeology. Wears a monocle and uses ten syllable words. Very thin.

Long Tom: Electrical expert. The physical weakling of the group, but a fast draw with a gun.

Ham: Harvard lawyer. Slender, handsome, quick moving. He never goes anywhere with out his razor sharp wit and razor tipped sword-cane.

Monk: Short, bald, hairy chested chemist and demolition expert. Lowbrow humor and earthy dialogue.

Each one of these guys had his own special weapon, his own style of dialogue and his own special talent. Whenever they needed to get past an alarm system, Long Tom was there. Whenever they needed to MacGuyver up an explosive device, Monk was there. When they came upon lost civilizations (they always did) Johnny was there. When they got hauled into court, or into a sword fight, Ham was there. If their plane crashed in the Arctic, you knew Renny could rebuild it and get them out of there before the polar bears attacked.

INTRODUCTIONS

In "The Professionals" (1966) Lee Marvin doesn't say, "we need another guy", he says: "What we really need is an equalizer. A dynamiter. A man with a delicate touch: to blow out a candle without putting a dent in the candle holder. And I know just the guy. He's not far from here...In jail." Burt Lancaster's character is introduced by his specific talent and weapon. Later we find out he's a well dressed romeo who can con his way into ANY woman's bed, and that he's had a few brushes with the law.

In my HBO film "Crash Dive!" I had to introduce some key members of the submarine crew who would become part of the hero's "team" later in the film. An earlier scene showed these guys at work, but I wanted the audience to get a feel for their personalities and backgrounds... to like them. The problem was, I only had a page and a half to introduce the team before the sub hijacking began.

How can you introduce six characters in a page and a half, and give the audience enough of their backstory to know them, be funny so that the audience likes them, yet not sound like exposition?

I came up with this answer:

EXT. USS ULYSSES - UNDER WATER

The submarine cruises under water.

INT. CONTROL ROOM — NIGHT

Lange moves from man to man, making sure they're on course. Everything is perfect, so he turns to MacDonald.

                    LANGE
          It's tradition for the Chief Of Boat to lead
          us in a sea shanty on our first night out.
          Murphy?

Murphy begins singing a bawdy sea shanty. Each of
our main characters takes center stage for a verse
which tells a little of their background. Everyone chimes in on the last line of each stanza.

                    MURPHY
          There was a young woman who lived by the
          sea, who had all the service boys scream
          ing. She dated the Army, Air Force, and
          Marines; but all she wanted was Sea Men.

                    ROBISON
          She met a young stud from the streets of
          L.A., and thought he was quite a he-man.
          Tried to get her to bed all night and all
          day...

                    EVERYONE
          But all she wanted was Sea Men.

                    DENT
          The son of a preacher tried to teach her to
          pray, but all he taught her was A-Men. He
          took her to church each and every Sunday...

                    EVERYONE
          But all she wanted was Sea Men.

                    WAGER
          A gambling man tried to teach her to play,
          but nothing could stop him from scheming.
          He bet her to win, and to show, and to
          stay...

                    EVERYONE
          But all she wanted was Sea Men.

INT. ENLISTED BUNKS — NIGHT
The laughter and singing echoes through the submarine.
The boat's maintenance man, the lowest enlisted
man onboard, LARRY BLOCK, is trying to sleep. A
twenty-something slacker who'd rather be playing
DOOM on his computer than trapped in a sub for
four months.

> BLOCK
> Hey, man, I'm trying to sleep down here.
> Sound like a bunch of goats.

INT. CONTROL ROOM — NIGHT
Collins hands the controls to YAMAGUCHI.

> COLLINS
> A hillbilly driver tried to give her a boat,
> and tried to be her dream man. Said he'd
> throw in the Chief, who's a crazy old goat...

> EVERYONE
> But all she wanted was Sea Men.

All the men laugh together. A true team. Only one
man in the Control Room isn't laughing, or even
smiling: MacDonald. He's too snobby to enjoy the
camaraderie.

> MURPHY
> This crazy old Chief was the son of a
> tailor, after looking at him she was
> screaming. To quiet the woman, he set her up
> with a sailor...

> EVERYONE
> But all she wanted was...
> (big finish) SEA MEN.

Lange smiles proudly at his men. He likes them. He
looks down at his locket, missing his family.

The sea shanty allowed each character to talk about themselves without sounding expositional. We know that Robison is a ladies man, that Murphy has self depreciating humor (he jokes about how ugly he is in his verse), that Collins is a "Hillbilly driver" which conjures up images of running moonshine, that Dent is religious, that Wager is willing to gamble, and shows us Block trying to escape the music. Because each gets his verse, the actor will get to use physical actions as well. Because the song had a punchline, the audience will laugh, and like these guys.

On the set, the director decided a song is a song... So he removed the sea shanty scene and substituted a rap number performed by extras which did nothing to illuminate character.

The critical members of the submarine's crew were never introduced. We know nothing about them when the submarine is hijacked, and have trouble telling them apart. This was further complicated by bad casting choices which de-ethnicized the crew. Three of the actors cast look almost identical in crew cuts and uniform.

How confusing!

ACCESSORIZING YOU TEAM

When you create your team members accentuate the differences between each team member. Is one a cowboy in western garb and another a flashy dresser in a $2,000 Italian suit? The cowboy will have different speech patterns than the clothes horse. The cowboy will listen to different music, have different points of reference, and use a different approach to problem solving than our man in Armani.

Each of the terrorists in "Crash Dive!" was given

their own weapon and their own point of view. A bad guy team. The female, Bolanne, wore a form fitting black suit with a bandoleer of throwing knives. One villain had a garrotte, another used a matched pair of pistols, a brutish ex-goatherd used a club and saw everything as "flock management"... Each villain had a distinctive weapon, look, and personality. The director removed these things from the film, making them just a bunch of bad guys.

On "Steel Sharks" I had to create a Navy SEAL team which Admiral Billy Dee Williams would send deep into enemy territory via Gary Busey's submarine. The problem here: the entire team would be dressed in identical uniforms, and then put on camouflage face paint... How can we tell them apart?

By "Accessorizing".

Whenever you have five soldiers, five bank robbers, or five doctors who all will be dressed the same, it's important to give each one a little something to tell them apart. An accessory... An "instant identifier".

Let's take five bank robbers dressed in identical blue suits and ski masks. Which is which? Give one a boutonniere, another a gold crucifix, a third gets a stop watch on a lanyard around her neck, a fourth wears dark glasses OVER the ski mask, the fifth wears a red cowboy bandanna around her neck. Instant identifiers! Now the audience can tell them apart at a glance.

Each "accessory" is also a way to show character. In my script for "Steel Sharks" I had a deeply religious character who always wore a crucifix, touching it sometimes during the mission. It was his touchstone, a great way to show his character, and was a physical way to tell him from the other guys when they were all dressed alike.

The tough, stern SEAL who would become the hero's mentor and surrogate father as the script progressed, wore a necklace of every bullet that ever hit him. This was a great symbol of the character's hardness, his invulnerability, and a way to instantly identify him. I had one of these "accessories" for each team member. A way to tell them apart and tell us about their character. The director didn't get it, and didn't use them. Try to tell these guys apart in the shoot outs now!

The more alike the characters look or dress, the stronger the accessory must be. Our five bank robbers in ski masks require big flamboyant accessories. The SEAL team in uniform and camouflage make up require big accessories. When we don't have the instant visual reference point of clothing style to tell characters apart, we need that something extra.

VIVA LA DIFFERENCE

All of your team members must be different. They must have different strengths and weaknesses. Different 'looks'. Different personalities and ways of handling problems. Different "voices" and speech rhythms. The audience must be able to instantly tell one from another.

All of these things must be planned out before you begin writing. If one of your characters is a Grand Prix racer, it'll probably change the outcome of your car chase if he's driving. Or create an interesting scene if he ends up in the backseat, and your fussy art expert is driving. A change in the outcome of the car chase changes EVERY scene which comes after it. So plan ahead! Make up a list of character traits for each team member. Contrast each Team Member with the Hero, and make sure there's plenty of contrast between each Team Member and the other members of the team, too. The more similar they are, the more different they must be!

TEAM EXAMPLE

In Paul Kyriazi's martial arts film "Weapons Of Death" (1981), each team member is given a specific weapon and a specific character arc. The story concerns the daughter of a wealthy family from San Francisco's Chinatown who is kidnaped by the Tongs.

The girl's brother, played by Eric Lee, assembles a team to rescue her from among his karate class friends: David, the bow and arrow expert, has trouble shooting at live targets. Eric, the swordsman, was stomped by the lead hench in Act 1. Josh, the lance expert, is opposed to killing. Paul, the gunslinger, is engaged to the girl the badguys have kidnaped. And Curt, who uses a Conan-sized broadsword is the girl's father... or maybe he isn't.

Each team member has a moment of truth in the film, where they must confront their personal demons to survive.

"Weapons Of Death" also uses a BAD GUY TEAM. A group of henchmen sent by the Villain to get the good guy team. Each member of the Bad Guy Team also has a special weapon and a special talent. This film is the most fun when it pairs off a Good Guy Team member with a lance against a Bad Guy Team member with a broadsword. There are dozens of fight styles and combinations you go through until the end of the film when each Good Guy Team member faces off against his Bad Guy Team counterpart: Two guys fighting with broadswords, or two guys in a high noon style pistol shootout. This a fun film which deserves a new video release.

DETAILS, DETAILS

Another device which pops up in team efforts is the conflict within a team. Alastair MacLean novels (and the films made from them like "The Guns Of Navarone" and "Where Eagles Dare") always have tension and dissention within the team.

From basic personality conflicts, to "one of us is a Nazi informer" subplots, conflict within a team keeps the scenes between car chases and shoot outs exciting, and adds another level of tension to the action scenes. Will Joe save Hal's life during the shoot out; when, in the preceding scene, Hal admitted that he'd slept with Joe's girl?

In "The Split" (1968) based on one of the Richard Stark novels by Don Westlake, a team of professional robbers are going to hit the LA Coliseum during a Rams playoff game. Tension in the team begins when a racist member played by Donald Sutherland locks horns with team leader Jim Brown. Each team member, Gene Hackman, Julie Harris, Ernest Borgnine, and Warren Oates, must choose sides in this racial debate.

A better team heist film with racial undertones is Nelson Gidding's "Odds Against Tomorrow". Racist Robert Ryan gets teamed with Harry Belafonte for a heist and can't seem to set aside his prejudices long enough to pull the job. When the robbery falls apart, they are forced to work together to survive.

"Odds Against Tomorrow" is a good example of how to incorporate a social message in a film which is non-stop action. This is a great film with a fantastic jazz score, based on a novel by William P. McGivern.

TODAY ON SPRINGER:
GOOD BAD GUYS, BAD GOOD GUYS

An extension of Team Conflicts is the GOOD BAD GUY and BAD GOOD GUY characters also found in MacLean films and books. In "Where Eagles Dare" we know that one of the good guys team is really a Nazi informer... But who? As the film plays out, we are given clues to the bad good guy's identity, but when it's finally revealed... it's still a good twist.

For a textbook example of how to use good bad guys and bad good guys, read Robert Rostand's "The Killer Elite". Three bodyguards are protecting an African Dignitary from three top assassins sent to kill him. But one of the assassins is providing anonymous tips to the good guys. And one of the three good guys is tipping off the bad guys. The resulting novel is filled with twists, turns, and thrill a minute action as our hero, Locken, tries to figure out which assassin he <u>shouldn't</u> kill... and which one of his two trusted sidekicks he <u>should</u> kill.

When they made the film version of this brilliant novel, screenwriter Sterling Silliphant removed the theme, plot, twists, and core of the novel; leaving a collection of action scenes which don't quite hang together. Hunt this book down and give it a read. You'll learn more about plotting action films than I have space to write in a dozen books. "The Killer Elite" is a classic action novel, ripe for a more faithful remake.

FUNERALS

As I said at the beginning of this chapter, Teams fill the role of sidekicks... and that means someone is going to die! Either at the end of Act 1 or the end of Act 2 (or both, if you have enough team members) one of the loyal, trusted, witty members of the team is going to get blown away.

In "The Professionals" the team is forced to shoot their horses to avoid discovery by Raza's army. Robert Ryan is given the task, but can't harm the innocent animals... This leads to Burt Lancaster's capture and torture at the end of Act 1. At the end of Act 2, Robert Ryan is wounded and the team must leave him behind to escape capture. Immediately after the team escapes, there is a silent "funeral" for Ryan... much like the one they held for Lancaster at the end of Act 1.

The funeral after a team member's death is a moment for the team to cast aside their differences and band together. It has the potential to be the most powerful moment of your film, the only time your macho action audience gets a little misty in the eyes. So milk it if you can! Make that funeral scene the most powerful scene in your script. Why? Because it's fun to see an audience of grown men cry.

Now that you know that every team has a leader, who is the film's hero, and the team members, who fill the obligations of the sidekick; and that every team member must be different in style, talent, weapon, speech, character, character arc, and look, you are ready to attempt a Team Effort script. But I would strongly suggest you write a dozen conventional action scripts before you try something as complicated as a Team Effort.

After you have finished your conventional action screenplay, you'll want to touch it up. Do a few rewrites. So in the next chapters we'll talk about avoiding cliches and coincidences, and polishing your script.

EXPLODING CLICHES

One of the major problems with beginners scripts is that they are filled with scenes we've seen before, rather than scenes we'd like to see. Readers frequently note predictability, lack of plot twists, and overly simplistic elements as the reasons why scripts are rejected. I think much of this is due to screenwriters who reprocess old films into new scripts, thereby keeping cliches alive.

My Websters defines a cliche as an oft repeated and tedious expression or idea. Boringly obvious and stale.

So, now that we have met the enemy, how may we vanquish him? I believe the best method is to use his own weapons against him. Once you have isolated the cliche, turn it upside down and backwards upon itself, transforming it into a twist or reversal.

Quentin Tarantino is famous for this. In his script "Reservoir Dogs" he gives us a group of macho, tough guy armed robbers. The tough guy cliche is: Once shot, they take it like a man. There are films where tough guys get shot, walk away, go home, and remove the bullet with a pocket knife and a pair of pliers, using whiskey (taken internally) as a pain killer.

Tarantino turns this cliche upside down by having the gut shot Mr. Orange screaming in pain in the back of the getaway car. Flipping the cliche even more, Tarantino has Mr. Orange begging for his partner, Mr. White, to "just hold me".

This is NOT cliche tough guy behavior. It is the exact OPPOSITE of how we expect tough guys to act. How does Mr. White react? Does he "put the wounded man out of his misery" like Pike does in "The Wild Bunch"... By killing him like a lame horse? No. Mr. White holds his hand.

When was the last time you saw a film were tough guys held hands? Tarantino, a movie junkie who knows every scene from every film ever made, is an expert at turning the oft repeated scenes on their heads to create something fresh and insightful. He does this by setting up the cliche, and just when the audience says to themselves "I know what's coming next", he gives them the exact opposite. Turning the cliche's weapons against itself.

The best way to deal with cliches is to:
1) KNOW THEM, 2) USE THEM, 3) TWIST THEM.

New cliches are born every day, and part of our responsibility as screenwriters is to know what the cliches are. This means you must be constantly studying films and reading scripts. If five screenwriters avoid the same cliche by the same method, it becomes a NEW cliche.

Cliched dialogue can either be a line we've hear too often, a line too "on the nose" for a scene, or a line which tell us what we see. No matter what, it is stale. Three good methods to deal with dialogue cliches are...

ONE: SAY THE OPPOSITE.

Here is the seduction scene from Ernest Lehman's "North By Northwest". Roger Thornhill, wanted for murder, is hiding in Eve Kendall's sleeping car.

```
                    THORNHILL
         I can't let you get involved. Too
         dangerous.

                    EVE
         I'm a big girl.

                    THORNHILL
         In all the right places, too.

                    EVE
         I mean, we've hardly met.

                    THORNHILL
         That's right.

                    EVE
         How do I know you aren't a murderer?

                    THORNHILL
         You don't.

                    EVE
         Maybe you're planning to murder me,
         right here, tonight.

                    THORNHILL
         Shall I?

                    EVE
         Yes... Please do...

This time, Eve's hands guide him, and it is a long
kiss, indeed.
```

This dialogue takes places during a passionate
embrace, and the exchange is broken by a number of
serious kisses. It certainly doesn't SOUND like the typi-

cal seduction patter, does it? Eve gives very good reasons NOT to sleep with Thornhill. Not to even allow him in her room. And Thornhill does NOTHING to relieve any actual fears she may have that he really is a killer. Instead of talking about sex, they talk about violence. "Maybe you're planning to murder me"? The opposite of what they are feeling.

I often wonder if this particular line began as a pun, but was changed by the censors. Thornhill is accused of STABBING his victim, and if Eve had said, "Maybe you're planning to STAB me, right here, tonight?" then Thornhill's reply would be a racy, delicious, come back.

TWO: FIND THE DETAILS.

Instead of having the character say what they feel, let them find a detail which illustrates their feelings. Have them talk about the detail, rather than the feelings.

In "Terms Of Endearment" Debra Winger tells Shirley MacLane that she will miss her by saying: "That is the first time I stopped hugging first."

When Bo Hopkins is asked to surrender by the Pinkerton Detectives in "The Wild Bunch", he doesn't just say "no", he says: "You can kiss my sister's black cat's ass." Surely the most memorable line in film history, and definitely too descriptive to be a cliche.

The key is to PERSONALIZE your dialogue with details from the character's life, which will not only get rid of the cliches, but offer insight and understanding of your character.

Though, I think we learned more than we wanted to about Bo Hopkins' character.

THREE: EXPLODE THE CLICHE.

This method requires that you find a cliche line and spin it to create witty variation in the tradition of Oscar Wilde and Dorothy Parker ("It was a divorce made in heaven", "If you laid all the girls from Vassar end to end, you won't have been the first").

"It's all over but the shouting" becomes "It's all over but the SHOOTING".
"She's the ROAD apple of my eye."
"I'm just going to play it by FEAR."
"He's a man of a thousand faces, but a master of none."
"She was at that SPENDER age."
"They gave him the benefit of his CLOUT."
"She never lets any grass grow under her BACK."

Your character might complain of always being "a NEIGHBOR of love." Or know a liposuction expert who "Let the fat out of the hag."

Yes, I admit these are all groaners, but these lines are no longer cliches.

No matter what method we may use, part of our duty as screenwriters is to keep our screenplays exciting and unusual, and the easiest way to do that is by avoiding cliches like the plague!

IT'S A SMALL WORLD

The pitch by a well known writer-director goes something like this: "World Heavyweight Champ Rocky Balboa is challenged by a boxer from Iraq, so he flies to the Middle East to take on Saddam's best fighter in an internationally televised match. The moment Rocky sees his opponent, he knows he's in trouble: This guy is HUGE. Big as a house. Trained from birth as a boxer. Rocky has little chance of winning.

"But he fights for America... and wins!

"Saddam gets mad, and has Rocky arrested and thrown into prison. The President Of The United States realizes the only way to be re-elected is to have Rocky Balboa rescued.... So he calls in the toughest commando ever to serve: John Rambo.

"Rambo fights his way into Iraq, and breaks Rocky out of prison... Where the two men realize that they are identical twins separated at birth! After bonding, the two long lost brothers fight together to escape Iraq and destroy Saddam's regime!"

Rocky and Rambo: Identical twins!
What a small world!
Motion pictures require us to suspend our disbelief. We know that Sylvester Stallone is not really Rocky Balboa, but an actor who gets $20 million per picture and has a thing for tall, beautiful, fashion models. If Stallone takes a punch, we know he doesn't really get

hurt. It's all make believe, and audiences are willing to spend $8 to sit in the dark and pretend.

But coincidence can lead to the death of suspension of disbelief. Wrenching the audience out of the "movie reality" and making them yell "Fake!" at the screen, or nudge their friends and say "Yeah, right" with epic sarcasm.

Though film is not a realistic medium, relying more on the rhythms and wild logic of dreams, the viewing audience is (hopefully) wide awake. So your script should give the appearance of realism. We perceive reality to be mostly free of coincidence. In fact, many coincidences which occur in real life would be considered unbelievable if transferred to the screen.

WANT TO GET LUCKY?

The reason audiences reject coincidence is because they reek of luck. In "Fled" the hand-cuffed heroes on the run grab a hostage... who has handcuff keys in her purse! What are the odds? The pretty hostage decides to help them escape the police, and even falls in love with one of the prisoners! Amazing luck! Later in the film, the two heroes are being chased... and find a pair of motorcycles with the keys in the ignition! These two should have skipped the action plot and flown to Vegas!

CAUSALITY IS REALITY

Websters defines coincidence as "A seemingly planned sequence of accidentally occurring events".

In real life, things don't happen for any particular reason. Accidents happen. Film reality should mimic the accidental feel of real life. The causality. When the audience leaves the theater, they don't feel hand of God moving them like chess pieces... they have free will. They create their own destiny. They want the characters on screen to have the same freedom. Take choice away from the characters with "planned accidents" and you have destroyed reality. You have forced situations to occur instead of allowing them to proceed naturally.

No matter how much planning has gone into your script, the audience should feel as if the events are occurring right before their eyes. In the theater they call this "The illusion of the first time". Even though the actors may have performed the play 300 times previously, when the Female Lead admits "I don't love you, I love your brother", the Male Lead should be shocked and heartbroken... as if this is the first time he's heard this, not the three hundred and first. The audience wants to believe every twist and reversal is happening right before their eyes... That they are WITNESS to these events.

As writers we may be playing our characters like puppets, but we don t want the audience to ever see the strings. We don't want our scripts to seem forced, manipulative. In our scripts one event should lead logically to the next, carrying the character along with it. Natural and uncontrived.

HOW MANY COINCIDENCES ARE TOO MANY?

Hey! Aren't you supposed to be allowed three coincidences in every script? I've heard three as the magic number from several newcomers to screenwriting and can only assume that college professors decided to pick a random number for amount of permissible coincidences. Why they all chose three is a coincidence.

If they were writing a script, that's the only one they could get away with.

One coincidence. That's the limit in every genre but comedy. Here's the bad news: it's used up by a coincidence we usually aren't even aware of.

Coincidence is inherent in story. Real life is vague, problems aren't solved, there is no 'plot'. By organizing incidents into a beginning, middle, and end with a protagonist and antagonist; you re already using up your allotment of coincidence. The inciting incident which launches your plot is the only coincidence an audience will let you get away with.

Everything else that happens in your script should be grounded in "reality" and seem coincidence-free. This includes both "good" and "bad" coincidences. Many writers eliminate "good" coincidences, then pile on the bad luck; creating dozens of coincidences which negatively impact the protagonist. Good idea, right? Wrong.

Too many bad coincidences provoke humor. Comics like Buster Keaton made an entire career out of playing protagonists with very bad luck. Terrible things happened to them for no apparent reason and WE LAUGH AT THE PREPOSTEROUSNESS OF THEIR MISFORTUNE. Nobody is that unlucky! So, unless you're writing a comedy like Joseph Minion's "After Hours", remember that too many bad coincidences is no different that too many good ones.

WHY? WHY? WHY?

The best way to remove coincidence is through motivation. There are really two types of coincidences: Forced and Casual. Forced coincidence is when we manipulate the story, playing God, to give a character amazing good luck (or amazing bad luck). Casual coincidence is when events occur in a logical, motivated way. Two characters who live in the same apartment building take the elevator at the same time. A minute either way and they would each have been on the elevator alone, so it's technically a coincidence. But the audience completely accepts it because it's how real life works. Had one character lived in New York and the other in Chicago, and they shared an elevator in California, that might be a forced coincidence... Unless it's a hotel elevator and they are attending the same business convention.

Motivation is the key to removing forced coincidence. Having a logical reason WHY things happen creates instant acceptance in the audience. Coincidence occurs when you haven't looked for the REASON why something might happen, but make it happen anyway. Pulling the strings on the puppets, instead of allowing your characters to get into trouble on their own for reasons the audience understands. Find the motives!

CAUSE AND EFFECT

For every action there is an equal and opposite reaction. When a ball hits the ground it bounces into the air, where gravity pulls it back to the ground so that it can bounce again. Our job is to trace the bouncing back to the hand that bounced it in the first place. The primary motivation. The ultimate WHY which has caused all of these incidents to occur. By knowing what set the ball into motion, you can remove all of the forced coincidence and replace it with motivation.

The best way to do this is to start your script with the primary motivation and build your story from the inside out. Coincidence often occurs when you re writing from the outside in. You come up with a great idea for an action scene on the Eiffel Tower, then find some excuse for your hero and villain to go to France.

Your excuse never seems real. But there are times when we need to reverse engineer a scene, to start with the effect and trace back to the cause. Make sure every event is grounded in motivation. Don't stop at the first bounce, keep going back until you find the primary motivator of your script. This event in this scene happened due to a domino run of events which usually begins with your script's inciting incident. The events are not coincidence, but an integral part of your overall story, often linked by theme.

Your script should be completely organic. Every action fully motivated, every effect traceable back to its cause. Most coincidence is sheer laziness on the part of the writer. Instead of tracing cause and effect back to find the motives by which the event could really happen, they opt for an easy way out.

There ARE no easy ways out.

MORE BROTHERS

My friend Don "The Dragon" Wilson did a film called "Bloodfist" about a kick boxer whose brother was killed in an illegal death match held in the Philippines. Don joins the contest to find his brother's killer and extract his revenge. Along the way he meets a beautiful girl... Her brother was ALSO killed in the death match, and she's ALSO looking for revenge. They team up, and find the killer... His motivation? His brother was killed in the death match! Every single character had a dead brother! Small world!

This is the sort of silly plotting that happens when

the motives are coincidences. This frequently happens in development, with Directors, Producers, and Devos who work from the outside in, assigning motivations rather than searching for them. Taking the lazy way out instead of doing the real work of writing - tracing back the effect to cause and primary motives. Instead of going with causality or motivations, they like to "make it personal" by ramming in an unbelievable coincidence. The audience always rejects these silly things.

In my original script to "Treacherous", the hero owns a resort and becomes involved with a sexy female guest... which gets him into trouble.

The director decided to make the sexy guest the hero's ex-girl friend which makes the action plot complete coincidence. It changed a believable situation where a total stranger stayed at a resort owned by the hero into the preposterous coincidence of having the guest who sets the plot into motion just happen to have known the hero in his previous occupation (and in a different country). Small World! I'm sure the director thought he was adding motivation, but he was actually using coincidence as motive. Removing the causality.

SCRIPT SPACKLE

Development folks often want motivations and explanations for random non-coincidental events. This isn't necessary. We have no idea why most things happen in the world. Everything doesn't need to be explained (by making it personal), as long as it makes sense or CAN make sense.

A "plot hole" is when a series of events doesn't make sense. When one event CAN NOT lead to the next. Unfortunately, the usual solution is to patch it with a liberal coat of "script spackle": A scene which plugs the hole using coincidence or fancy footwork on the part of the writer. Instead of solving the story problem, they've covered the hole and hope nobody notices. I've seen screenplays with more script spackle than script! This is solving a problem from the outside in, instead of from the inside out.

Beware of "false plot holes"!

I've have Devos point out supposed "plot holes" which were actually non-coincidental causality. Things which DID make sense on examination, they just didn't examine them long enough. If the audience knows the situation CAN happen (is realistic) that's all that really matters. To "fix" a false plot hole by adding script spackle DAMAGES the script rather than improves it.

NOTHING PERSONAL

Devos like to make all motivations personal, but everyone can't have a dead brother. It's a mistake to change a believable causality for overly motivated characterization. Some characters are okay just doing their jobs.

The FBI's top serial killer expert is called in to stop a crazed killer hacking up college students. Hero shows up at the crime scene, only to discover the latest victim is his own daughter!

You might think giving him two motivations is better than one, but it actually creates a "forced coincidence". Of all the college students in the world, how could the killer possibly get the only one related to the FBI's top serial killer expert? What are the odds? This is the sort of thing which provokes laughter in the audience... It's ironic humor, after all.

A motivation can be either personal or a franchise, but it can't be both without becoming coincidence. Having two unrelated reasons to be involved in the story is unbelievable. Being the FBI's top serial killer expert is enough.

In Thomas Rickman's "The Laughing Policeman" Walter Matthau plays a detective who becomes personally involved in his work. The unsolved murder of a little boy still haunts him years later. Being a detective gives him more than enough motivation to solve the case. He cares about his job, we care about him, we care about his job.
That's why it doesn't need to be personal.

NOT MY JOB

The reverse is also true. If the lead's connection to the story is personal, he shouldn't also be an expert in the very subject the story revolves around.

In "Die Hard" John McClane isn't an anti-terrorist expert in a building taken over by terrorists, he's a simple New York beat cop used to checking bad IDs and busting petty crooks. He only has a personal motivation, not a franchise; the only coincidence is inciting incident.

"Lethal Weapon 2" has a fairly believable story about our buddy cops trying to bust a South African crime syndicate, but loses all credibility at the end when we find out the scumbags they're chasing are... coincidentally... the same ones who killed Mel Gibson's wife! (long before the first film begins). Small world!

IS THERE A LION TAMER IN THE HOUSE?

I read an unsold script about a tough cop on the trail of a mad bomber. Early in the script we find out the cop's hobby is mountain climbing. The writer made a big deal out of it, devoting an entire scene to the cop explaining pitons, crampons, and climbing techniques. The cop chases the mad bomber through New York, where he's blowing up really tall buildings.

Then, three quarters of the way through the script, the mad bomber traps the cop on the roof of a very tall building with a ticking bomb! Of course, the cop uses his mountain climbing knowledge to climb down the side of the building and escape the blast. Lucky coincidence: the cop's hobby being mountain climbing. If he'd taken up golf, he'd never have survived.

No matter how well you "set up" a coincidence, it's STILL a coincidence. You can spend twenty pages showing how much this cop loves mountain climbing, but the coincidence remains. This was lazy writing. The writer painted himself into a corner, came up with the mountain climbing escape, then went back and planted it in an earlier scene... Working from the outside in, instead of the inside out. Creating coincidences instead of causality.

The key to removing coincidence is motivation and working from the inside out. Finding the cause which creates the effect. Creating dreams which the audience can view while wide awake.

SLIGHTLY OUT OF FOCUS

You may think that the focus of a film is the Director Of Photography's responsibility, something which happens on the film set, and far away from your desk... But focus begins with the screenplay.

Here's an example: Two characters are in the same shot, but at different focal lengths. The Director Of Photography must choose which character will be in focus. His decision will be based on what's in the script. Your script.

Though the creative process may be wild, byzantine and scatter shot, the results of that creation should be tightly focused, somewhat linear, and easy to understand. Screenplays are simple stories about complex people. Problems frequently arise when the wild imagination must be tamed to fit the rigid structure of the screenplay. It's like trying to return the spring snakes to the tin after they have erupted on the unsuspecting victim: You know they'll fit back in the can, but squeezing them in there seems impossible.

THE FIRST STEP:
In focusing your script is to know what your screenplay is about. This seems simple enough, but many times when I ask a writer to tell me about their script, they

answer with a disjointed, rambling monologue which leaves me more confused than enlightened. Each piece is well described, but I'm not sure how they all fit together into a single story.

Try this: Tell a friend what your script is about using no more than three brief sentences. (Remember, TV Guide will only use one brief sentence when your film hits cable.) Can you relate the entire idea of the script to them? Will they understand who the lead character is, and what their goals and conflicts will be? If you have trouble telling a friend what your story is about, imagine how much trouble a development exec who has given your script a quick read over the weekend will have telling your story to the producer with the keys to the checkbook.

THE SECOND STEP:

Who is your lead character? Once the producer buys your script, he's going to spend $14-20 million for the star of the film; then hire some character actors or secondary names like Gene Hackman, Samuel Jackson, or Bonnie Bedelia at $2 million to $500,000 for the rest of the roles.

Is it obvious when reading your script who gets the $20 million? It's only ONE character, and the script will be about THAT character being forced to confront and solve an INTERNAL CONFLICT (character arc) in order to solve an EXTERNAL CONFLICT (plot).

This is the character who will be in focus when the Director Of Photography is faced with a focal length decision. As Canadian screenwriter Matthew Cope says: "The camera follows the money."

That lead character needs to be in about 75% of the movie (it's called "Face Time" in the biz). The producer wants to get her $20 million worth, and it costs the same if Stallone is in ten scenes or every scene. Your script is going to be ABOUT the lead character's problems, so it only makes sense that he's in as much of the film as possible. The producer will insist on it.

In William Goldman's "Adventures In The Screen Trade", he has an entire chapter on "Protecting The Star". This is some of the most important information you'll find in any screenwriting book, and required reading. Mr. Goldman says, "There is no single more important commercial element in screenplay writing than the star part". The star part, the lead character, is the focus of the film. Any other character is expendable. You've got to know who is getting the $20 million, and make sure they are in the majority of the film.

THE THIRD STEP:

Are the objectives of your lead character easy to understand? Your lead character is setting out to DO SOMETHING. Attain a specific goal.

In William Goldman's "Ghost And The Darkness" Val Kilmer's character is trying to build a bridge across a river in Africa. The audience can easily understand building the bridge. Are the objectives physical? Concrete? A vague goal like World Peace won't work. Film is a visual medium, and the goal needs to be something we can see.

In "Ghost And The Darkness", it's that bridge. We can see the river, and the end of the railroad tracks on either side. By the end of the film, we can see the result of Kilmer's character's objectives: The bridge spanning the river, connecting the two sets of tracks.

In "The Fugitive", Dr. Richard Kimble is searching for the One Armed Man who killed his wife.

A specific person. We can SEE that he has only one arm, and SEE that he is the same man Kimble fought with at the murder scene.

It would not be enough to have Kimble's goal just be to evade the police. That's not concrete enough. Not visual. How can we tell he's evaded the police? The lead character's goal has to be something the Director Of Photography can focus his camera on. Something we can see. One single thing.

THE FOURTH STEP:

The path to your lead character's objectives should be linear. A single straight line leading from where the character is now, to where the character wishes to be. NOT a complicated series of events like the old "Mouse Trap" board game.

I call this the A-B-C of the script. Does each scene lead logically to the next scene along the path to the lead character's objectives? The lead character has to find the quickest and most direct route to her goals. It shouldn't involve a bunch of little side trips, or too many back roads.

In "The Fugitive" script, Kimble becomes involved with a pretty doctor (played by Julianne Moore in the film). This entire subplot was filmed, but unused because it distracted from the linear movement of the film. Kimble gets no closer to his goals through this relationship, and it actually distracts him from his objectives. "The Fugitive" remains tightly focused on the capture of the One Armed Man, and is successful because side trips like the romantic subplot were eliminated.

We EXPECT conflicts along the way to take the lead character off course, but we also expect Dr. Richard Kimble to capture a One Armed Man at the end of "The Fugitive", not become involved with the problems of a Red Headed Woman, no matter how attractive she may be. The lead character's objectives must remain a constant no matter how many variables the plot (and antagonist) throw in her way.

In "Ghost And The Darkness", the lions keep eating the workers, taking Val Kilmer's bridge building objectives off course. Kilmer hunts the lions and sets traps for them. Why? So that he can get back to work building his bridge!

THE FIFTH STEP:

The way to keep your lead character focused is to know her PLAN OF ACTION. No matter how many times the antagonist tries to knock your hero off her path, she must always maintain that plan of action.

Every time she's slammed off course, she has to pick herself up, dust herself off, and start down that road again. Even if she gets hit so hard she's dizzy, she still needs to know exactly where she's going, and what she is going to do next. The only exception is if indecision is part of her character arc, and I strongly caution against that. People don't spend $8 to see wishy-washy heroes. They want to see strong, take-charge type people. We see enough indecisive people in everyday life, why would we want to PAY to see more of them?

STEP NUMBER SIX:

When the hero's plan of action just doesn't work, she should come up with a new plan, based on the same objectives, almost instantly. There are times when your hero is going to pick the route to her objectives, only to find the road closed for repairs. What seemed like the quickest and most direct way to obtain her goals was a major mistake, and may even cause pain and loss for your hero.

When this happens, remember that the audience's "fidget clock" is ticking. If your hero can't get over her loss and get back on track with a new plan to obtain her goals, your story will lose precious momentum, and some audience members may take this as an invitation to visit the candy counter or rest room.

We don't want that. One of our goals is to keep the audience in their seats, even if their bladders are about to burst. An audience in the bathroom is NOT watching your film.

THE SEVENTH STEP:

Is to know who your antagonist is, and what his objectives and plan of action are. Everything I've said about your lead character's objectives goes double for the antagonist. Though your hero may have to abandon her plan of action, the villain's plan of action will always remain an unchanging constant. An out of control bus knocking over anything in its path.

In Graham Yost's "Speed" Dennis Hopper is going to blow things up until he gets his money. He starts with an elevator. When that doesn't work, he tries a city bus or two. When they set a trap for him, he goes so far as to strap explosives to HIMSELF in order to get the money he feels he deserves. The quest for the money by using explosives is a constant for the villain. He never changes that plan, even though Keanu Reeves' smart young bomb squad guy does everything possible to stop him.

The villain is focused to the point of tunnel vision, and the bomb squad cop must force Hopper (and a subway car) out of that tunnel in order to stop him.

In the end, the hero will become more focused on her goal than the villain, and that's how she survives and conquers.

BABY STEPS:

The Director Of Photography can light and focus for many different depths of field; from deep focus, to a macro where only a pin head will be in focus. There are times when we do this in our scripts as well.

Every once in a while, I get "caught in a whirlwind". A dozen things happen to me at the same time, and I lose track of my goals. The day comes to an end, and I haven't written any pages on my script. I feel like that guy who used to spin plates on the tips of pool cues on the Ed Sullivan show, running from one small emergency to the next but never getting anything done.

This happens frequently to protagonists in action scripts and farce comedies. They can get caught in the whirlwind of a scene; lots of action, but they end up exactly where they started out.

You can remedy this with a method I call Baby Steps. The key is to give your protagonist small goals within the scene which combine into the larger goal of solving the current problems and moving your lead into the next scene. It's a bunch of baby steps which get the character across the room.

In a wild action sequence, this might be: "If I can only get that fallen gun... I can shoot the guy on the platform... run past the three guards in the confusion... shoot them if I have to... and get out that door." This is a plan of action which will let your hero escape (whether it works or not is another thing entirely).

But the audience (and reader) must be able to see the plan of action step by step and understand it. Even if they can't see the entire plan, there must be small understandable goals which build to a solution. This gives your hero purpose within the scene. Your protagonist must always be actively DOING SOMETHING to get out of whatever scrape you've put her in.

WATCH YOUR STEP!

Suspense scenes are based on a "focus object" which the suspense revolves around. I touched on this in my "Secrets" chapter earlier, but here's another example.

In my cable film "Hard Evidence" there is a scene where our businessman hero and his drug running girl friend have to cross a border with $4 million in cash and heroin in a suitcase. Now, this case is specially designed to pass through an ex-ray machine, but the minute a Customs Agent opens it, my hero is in jail for the rest of his life. In the script, they fly into LA and go through the customs line at the airport.

As they wait their turn, suspense builds. Someone in front of them has their luggage searched. Their bag gets closer and closer to the Customs Agent. Tension. Their turn. The Customs Agent examines the suitcase exterior and asks them questions. His fingers move to the latches... will he open it? The girlfriend makes a joke, the Customs Agent smiles, and passes them through without opening their luggage.

In a story conference, one of the producers wanted to change the location from the airport to a drive through check point.... they had a beautiful one they could get for the film. I argued: The focus of the scene needs to be the suitcase filled with drugs and money. If we drive a car through the checkpoint, the focus becomes the

CAR. The Customs Agent will want to search the trunk, check to see if anything is hidden in the spare tire, and feel the seats for suspicious lumps. Sure, he might search the suitcase, but it's one of SEVERAL items in his search, not the FOCUS of his search.

The producer ended up agreeing with me that the airport scenario was better than the check point, even if the location wasn't as exciting. The scene as written was focused and suspenseful.

THE TENTH STEP:

Make sure each individual scene is focused on the objectives of the script. The small objectives have to lead to the big objectives.

Think of your script as a house of cards. Each scene is a card. If you can remove any scene, and the house remains standing, that scene shouldn't have been in your script.

DNA

Not only should each scene move the story forward, each scene should also be a microcosm of the story. Every scene should contain the DNA necessary to clone the entire script.

You should be able to read any scene from your script and have some idea of what the script is about. This is another part of Organic Screenwriting - Each scene has to be an integral part of the script, not just a bunch of filler. The scene should expose character, move the story forward, and deal with the lead character's Inner and Outer conflicts. Long rambling scenes which take forever to make their points need to be cut to their essence... which includes the script's DNA.

CURLY SAYS IT ALL:

In Lowell Ganz and Babaloo Mandel's comedy "City Slickers", Curly (played by Jack Palance) explains the secret of life to Mitch (Billy Crystal):

```
                    CURLY
          You know what the secret of life is?


                    MITCH
                  (intrigued)
          No, what?

Curly STICKS UP his index FINGER.

                    CURLY
          This.


                    MITCH
          Your finger?


                    CURLY
          One thing. Just one thing.  You
          stick to that... and everything
          else don't mean shit.
```

The secret of life, and the secret of writing a good script... Bering able to focus on your goals, focus on your story, focus on your work. Just one thing at a time.

SIXTEEN STEPS TO BETTER DESCRIPTION

There are dozens of books, seminars, classes, and articles available on how to improve your screenplay's dialogue. By now your lines should have the pluck of Parker, the bite of Benchley and the soul of Steve Zallian. Every line of dialogue you write is brilliant. But film is a visual medium, and your script will probably have more description than dialogue. Much more.

Readers frequently complain about too much black stuff (description) and reject scripts for being dense and verbose (description again!). What can we do to improve the writing that comes between those brilliant lines?

THE WORD IS ACTION

My first step is easy: Don't think of it as DE-SCRIPTION, think of it as ACTION. Movement. Things happening. Describing a stationary object is not only boring, it's probably not necessary. The Production Designer will decide the floor plan of the house, the Set Decorator will decide how to furnish it, the Prop Master will add the details like family photos and nick-knacks. It's not our job as writers to describe any of this stuff (unless it's REQUIRED by the plot).

If the slug line says: INT. JOE'S LIVING ROOM - DAY, the reader will imagine a sofa, some chairs, a TV, and most of the details. We don't have to mention them. Our job isn't to paint the whole picture, just give the absolute minimum amount of information required to set the location.

Sometimes, the slug line does it all. Which means what comes after the slug line is ACTION. I use the "Script Thing" program, and that's what it calls the element between patches of dialogue. We are writing MOTION pictures, and what we are describing is people and objects MOVING.

So the first step is to remember you aren't describing THINGS you are describing THINGS HAPPENING. When we use our words to paint pictures, we aren't painting still lifes.

THE DEVIL IS IN THE DETAILS

There are times when INT. JOE'S LIVING ROOM - DAY is too generic. The reader needs additional information. The trick is not to bore the reader by completely describing the living room. Instead, find the one or two details which give us clue to the rest, and let the reader's imagination fill in the rest.

```
INT. JOE'S LIVING ROOM - DAY
Pizza boxes and empty beer cans litter the floor.

INT. JOE'S LIVING ROOM - DAY
A vase of fresh cut flowers on a doily atop the
piano.
```

Two very different living rooms. How is the style of furniture in the first room different than that in the second? Imagine a lamp in the first room... it's different than the lamp you would imagine in the second room. The carpet is different. The curtains are different. I imagine posters thumb tacked to the walls in the first room, and carefully framed fine art lithos in the second.

They key is to carefully choose a detail which implies other details. To find an example or metaphor which sums up the entire location. That way you can describe an entire room in one short sentence.
Notice that this gives us clues to character as well. These are two VERY different Joes!

HIDDEN DESCRIPTIONS

If we combine the first two steps, we come up with a third. The best place to hide a description is within action. Instead of a boring static image, give the reader an exciting bit of action and sneak in a little description along the way.

```
INT. JOE'S LIVING ROOM - DAY
Joe brushes away old pizza boxes, plops down on
the sofa.
```

The reader is focusing on Joe, and doesn't even notice you slip in the description of the living room. No static writing, no still life feel.
Economical writing which manages to do three things at the same time: Show things happening, describe the location, and illuminate character.

WESTERN UNION

Screenwriting is distilled writing. Using the fewest number of words to create the greatest possible impact. Novelists can spend pages describing something in minute detail (Proust wrote seven volumes on a fellow eating a cookie and remembering his past), but we've got no more than 120 pages to get our entire story across.

Economical writing is probably the most important part of our job... And the most difficult part. But how do you get rid of flabby, lazy writing? How do you fight the writer's natural tendency to be verbose? One of my tricks is to imagine I'm sending a telegram at 35 cents a word, and I've only got $2 and change in my pocket. Instead of splashing words on the page, I have to pick each word carefully. Relate the maximum message for the minimum price.

Screenwriting is similar to Haiku, you have a limited number of words to paint your picture. The trick is tho chose words which IMPLY other words. Words which can not only carry their own weight, but are strong enough to carry entire ideas and/or images.

If there's an art to screenwriting, it's knowing how to pick strong but simple words. Either while writing, or rewriting, I will take every sentence and try to find a more succinct way of relaying the information. In first drafts, I might use a half dozen words to do the same job a single word can do, or use extraneous words, or beat around the bush instead of finding a direct route to what I'm trying to say. By imagining each sentence as part of a telegram (charged by the word) I decide exactly what I want to say and figure out the briefest way to say it.

CHOOSE YOUR WORDS CAREFULLY, MR. BOND

The key to economical writing is word choice. I

may splash words on the page for my first draft, but while rewriting I try to find the EXACT word to match the situation.

This accomplishes two things at once: creates quick, easy to read sentences... which have greater impact than their flabby counterparts. Joe walks into the room. Walks is too generic. There are probably a hundred synonyms for walk, each describing a distinctive type of ambulation.

If Joe saunters in, strides in, struts in, strolls in, marches in, paces in, or bounces in; not only does this give us a specific type of walk, but adds to the action and character while removing boring overused words from your script.

ONCE MORE, WITH FEELING

Another trick is not to describe how something LOOKS, but how it FEELS. The Production Designer will decide what a room looks like, the Casting Director will decide what a character looks like... That leaves us describing ATTITUDES.

The script I just finished, "Hard Return", takes place in the future. Instead of trying to describe an entire futuristic world, I used these sixteen steps to give the reader a quick impression, allowing the reader's imagination to fill in the rest.

```
EXT. URBAN JUNGLE, 2019 AD — EVENING

The wreckage of civilization.
Crumbled  buildings, burned  out  cars, streets
pockmarked by war. Downed power lines arc and
spark on the street.
This place makes Hell look like Beverly Hills...
Except the battered twisted metal sign reads
"Beverly Hills".
```

```
Night is falling.  Fingers of shadow reaching out
to grab anyone foolish enough to be in this part
of town.
```

That's the only time my future world is described in the script. Slug lines and action take it from here. Between the arcing and sparking power lines and the fingers of shadow I show you how the future FEELS... frightening, ugly, dangerous.

A LITTLE POETRY

Goes a long ways. Using imagery, alliteration, homonyms and other forms of word play helps spice up your descriptions, but use them sparingly. Too much poetry reeks of cutesy writing . Writing asides to the reader is also "too cutsey". Shane Black can get away with it, but chances are the rest of us can't. Remember, our job is to involve the reader in the story... Not jerk them out of it with wry asides or amusing allusions. Your writing should be both interesting and invisible, which means the word play should service the script, not show what a clever writer you are.

BLACK STUFF

An easy step for getting rid of dense black stuff is to remember the Four Line Rule. No passage of action should last longer than four lines.   If you have a big action scene, which lasts a page or more... break it up with spaces! Every four lines, put in a blank line. This instantly adds more white stuff to your script! Another quick trick for long action passages is to have at least one line of dialogue on every page... even if it s just a charac-ter yelling "Watch out!"   This breaks up the page, and gives the reader a break from reading actions described.

STYLE ON THE PAGE

The best way to make descriptions easy to read is to make them FUN to read. To create the excitement you envision on the screen, right on the page. Develop your own personal style of writing action passages.

Style breaks up the page and makes your writing distinctive. Using sounds like "BLAM!" or "CLANG!" Writing single sentence action blocks.
One.
Word.
Sentences.
Which.
Draw.
The.
Reader.
Down.
The.
Page.

Anything that makes the script more exciting to read, and involves the reader in the action. Experiment. After a few scripts, you will develop your own style and your own 'voice' in descriptions. Developing a 'voice' is an important step in taking command of the page (more on that, later).

CHARACTER

Do you think you could completely describe a character in four words? Lawrence Kasdan managed that amazing feat in his script for Body Heat . This is one of the best examples of clear, succinct writing I have ever read. "Teddy Laurson, rock and roll arsonist". Kasdan manages to convey Teddy's occupation and attitude which allows us to imagine details about everything from number of tattoos to hair length and personal grooming to wardrobe in ONLY FOUR WORDS!

If he can do it, so can the rest of us.

In my script "Heart Of Glass" I described Lt. Bobby Mazeppa as a "Beach boy homicide detective".

Your turn.

ACTIVE WORDS

A basic, but I've read dozens of scripts which would have been greatly improved had the writers stayed awake in their high school English classes when the teacher said: "Use active verbs. Joe doesn't TRY to sit on the sofa, he SITS on the sofa".

In fact, he PLOPS DOWN on the sofa.

"Try" is a weasel verb... it takes the power from the active verb. ("starts to", "begins to", and "ing": WALKS is stronger than walking.)

Beware of the "To Be" verbs, there is no action in a "To Be" sentence like this one!

KILL THE WIDOWS!

In the wonderful world of typesetting, when the last word of a sentence carries over onto a new line of print it s called a widow . A single word which takes up an entire line of space. How wasteful!

I always do a rewrite to kill all of the widows. If one or two words from the end of a sentence end up taking up an entire line, I rework the sentence until I can get it to fit entirely on one line. My goal is a widow-free script. Not only does this force me to choose the correct words, eliminate useless or fatty words, and write clear, concise sentences; it also trims my script, allowing room for more important elements.

And the script looks cleaner on the page!

NO BUTS!

The easiest two words to trim out of a sentence are AND and BUT. Usually these words are completely unnecessary. Cut them.

CONFIDENCE

Know what every sentence and every word means, and write clear enough so that anyone who reads your script understands what you have written. Write strong sentences and strong images.

Remember: You command the page. You control the words. You control the reader. This is writing with confidence.

A reader friend of mine frequently complains about writers who don't command the page. They seem unsure of what they're writing, filling their script with weasel verbs and beating around the bush with long, run on sentences. Don't fall into that trap. Know what you're going to write, write it.

YOU are in control of your script.

PAGE TURNERS

Not Paige Turco, that beautiful actress from "NYPD Blue" and "Party Of Five", but page TURNERS.

Little cliff hangers at the end of your page which force the reader to turn to the next page. I have been known to add extra spaces or trim entire lines just to end a page on a moment of suspense.

If there s a moment where the hero is about to be killed but saves himself, I want the "about to be killed" part at the end of one page so you have to turn the page and keep reading to get to the "saves himself" part.

In fact, I've even added artificial suspense to the end of a page to keep those pages turning.

One of my thriller scripts had a scene where the hero comes home, and his girlfriend suggests they go out to dinner. Boring!

The hero enters his apartment on the second to last line on the page... So I added "Hands reach out from behind the door and grab him!"

(page ends).

At the top of the next page, we find out it's his girlfriend. Lines like this not only turn your script into a page turner, they add suspense, reversals, and excitement.

Fifteen different ways to make your descriptions as exciting as your dialogue. I've saved the most important step for last: If you think your description could use a little trimming, take a chainsaw to it. Cut without mercy. Most of us are so in love with our own words that we don't cut enough.

Remember: Your writing can never be too lean or too exciting.

FINISHING TOUCHES

Writing "THE END" is usually only the beginning. Once you've finished writing your action script, go out and celebrate, but DON'T send our script to a producer. It probably needs a rewrite or two.

Every script can be improved, and our job as writers is to get our scripts as close to perfect as possible before we try to sell them. Remember, you may only get one chance in a lifetime to have a Producer read your action script, so you want to make sure they read the BEST script possible.

My advice is to shelve your first action script and begin writing another one right away. Once that second script is finished, THEN go back to rewrite the first. Why? You'd be surprised at how often something which made sense while you were writing it, looks silly a few months later.

It's like the old joke about the writer who keeps waking up in the middle of the night with great story ideas, but by the next morning he couldn't remember them. He was sure that if he used one of those story ideas, he could write a hit film. So he put a pad and pen next to his bed. He woke up in the middle of the night with an amazing idea, and wrote it down.

The next morning when he got up, he remembered the great idea and grabbed his note pad. Written on it was "Boy meets girl".

When you finish writing your second script and come back to rewrite the first one, you may find that some of it is "Boy meets girl". The following are some things to think about when rewriting your script.

RESEARCH

In action scripts, bad research can be fatal... at least to your hero. Here's an example: Your hero has a 44 magnum, your villain has a 30-06 rifle. They stand 500 yards away from each other and fire. Bang! Bang!

Bad research just killed your hero. Even though his 44 magnum is the most powerful handgun in the world, 500 yards is out of its effective range. The heavy (240 grain) bullet will drop 273 inches below the target... But the hero is well within range of the villain's 30-06.

The more research you do before you write your script, the less rewriting you will have to do later, when you find out that correcting a simple research error means you've just killed your hero. Know the facts and double check them before you begin writing your script.

I've written a couple of films which were made with Navy/Department Of Defense approval. The key to obtaining approval (which allowed the producers to film on an actual aircraft carrier during manuevers... for free!) is a factually accurate script. You have to get the details perfect. All it takes is a little reading.

When it's time to do your rewrite, go back over your facts and make sure they're accurate. Give a copy of your script to someone with the technical knowledge covered in the plot. Have them read it and point out any errors, or supply any neat ideas you may have missed. Every fact opens a door to exciting story possibilities.

When a producer or development executive reads your script, here are a few things they'll be looking at.

1) Does your script have an interesting, exciting plot? Something we haven't seen before? Is it logical and possible? Is it executed in an exciting manner?

2) Can you easily condense your plot into a single sentence "log line"? When the development executive pitches your script to her boss, she'll have to sum it up in one or two sentences. If YOU can't do it, how can you expect her to do it?

3) Does your theme explore a hidden need of the audience (using the "plot seed" theory)?

4) Is the Villain's plan well motivated? Does it threaten others? Is it believable?

5) Does your hero belong in this script? Is HE/SHE the most logical one to stop the villain?

6) Is your hero well motivated? Does your hero "grow" throughout the script? (character arc)

7) Does your character have a compelling inner struggle? Is there "rooting interest"?

8) Is the first page exciting? Professional readers say they can tell by the end of the first page if the script will make a good film. So make sure your first page knocks their socks off.

9) The same readers say that by the ten page mark, they've usually made their decision to recommend the script or not. So use those first ten pages to set up your conflict, and thrust your hero into peril.

10) Do you have strong act enders, which thrust your story into a new and exciting direction?

11) Is there an emotional mid-point tied into your character's inner struggle?

12) Does your third act really blow the roof off? Is it wall to wall action, out of the fry pan into the fire?

13) Is there a satisfying resolution where the hero vanquishes the villain?

14) Does your script tell its story VISUALLY? Is it about people DOING THINGS?

15) Is there a whammo every ten pages?

16) Have you used an economy of words in your description? Remember to make EVERY word count. Imagine your script is a telegram, and every word is going to cost you. Your job is to use as FEW words to relate MAXIMUM information. Trim EVERY word you can. And use the EXACT, RIGHT WORD, not second best.

17) Is your action description exciting? Will a reader want to skip over the dialogue to get to the next passage of action?

18) Are there twists, reversals, and rugpulls? Is your script unpredictable?

19) Is there suspense? Cross cutting? Big clocks and scene clocks?

20) Do your plants payoff? If there's a sword on the wall in Act 1, it has to be used by Act 3. If Q gives James Bond a parasol that shoots poison gas, it's required that Bond use it by the end of the film. You've got to tie up all the lose ends (logically) by the end of the film.

21) Are ALL of your characters well motivated? Even the walk ons? Are their actions logical?

22) Is your script free of coincidence?

23) Do each of your characters have unique voices and speech patterns, so that they can be identified by their dialogue, even if the characters headings are covered? Many readers WILL do this to your script. Be prepared. Different characters have different vocabularies!

24) Is your dialogue snappy? Witty? Go over EVERY line and see if you can improve it.

25) Do you have an "echo line", which forms a nexus between the hero's inner problem and outer problem? Does the meaning of the echo line change as the hero grows? For more information on echo lines, see Michael Hauge's "Writing Screenplays That Sell" page 98-99.

26) Is there a "take home line" in your script? A line so clever that the audience will repeat it the next day at work? "Go ahead, make my day." "I'll be back." "Do you feel lucky, punk?"

27) Is there a payback line?

28) Did you bridge your scenes with overlapping dialogue or visual match cuts? For more information on match cuts and bridges, see Sheldon Tromberg's "Making Money Making Movies" page 26-29.

29) Does each individual scene move the story forward? Does each scene contribute to the whole? Does each scene contain suspense, reversals, and PUNCH?
Go through your script SCENE BY SCENE, looking at the micro, the DNA, and rewrite it.

30) Once your script is rewritten, give it to a half dozen other screenwriters and ask for their input. Listen to what they have to say, then rewrite your script . When you think your script is close to perfect, then and only then, send it to a producer or agent.

Action films are the most popular genre in the world, with plenty of opportunity for talented new screenwriters. It worked for me. My first produced screenplay was as action film released in 1984. Since then, I've earned a reasonably good living writing action and thriller scripts... Seventeen produced features as I write this!

By using the inside information in this book, you can write a salable action script.
Now it's time for YOU to swing into action, and get to work on your script. Set aside a couple of hours a day to work at your computer. Remember, it's only one page at a time. If you only write one page a day, seven days a week, you'll have a completed first draft in about three months. THREE MONTHS! You can write a page a day, right? So start tomorrow, and three months from now, you'll have a new, exciting action script... Maybe the next "Face/Off" or "Die Hard"!

DIE HARD ANALYSIS

Since its release in 1988, "Die Hard" has become a benchmark of action films, frequently sighted as one of the best action films of the past twenty years. The film has also become part of Hollywood vocabulary, used to describe other films: "Die Hard" at the Stanley Cup. "Die Hard" on a bus. "Die Hard" on a warship. "Die Hard" on a plane. "Die Hard" in a hospital. "Die Hard" on a train. "Die Hard" in a luxury condo complex. And "Die Hard" on a submarine (my HBO film "Crash Dive!").

Why has this film received such an elevated degree of recognition and respect? The answer lies in the multi layered characters and complex-yet-organic script by Jeb Stuart and Steven E. deSouza. Every nuance, every twist and reversal, every shading of character is spelled out on the page; making "Die Hard" the ideal learning screenplay for the action genre.

But first a little history. "Die Hard" began life as a sequel to another movie. In 1968, Roderick Thorp's best selling novel "The Detective" had been made into a film starring Frank Sinatra and Lee Remick, released by 20th Century Fox. When the film became a hit, the producers told Thorp if he wrote a sequel, they would buy it. Thorp's response was "I'm writing one now." Then he went home and started writing a new chapter in the life of the detective played by Frank Sinatra. He had read a book titled "The Glass Tower" (which would eventually be made into the film "The Towering Inferno") about a group of people trapped on the top floor of a high rise office building by a raging fire, and found the idea of people trapped above the reach of rescue equipment intriguing.

In that time period newspaper headlines seldom reported fires. What they did report was civil unrest, the latest bombings by the Weather Underground, and the latest kidnapping or bank robbery committed by the Red Army terrorist group. So Thorp substituted terrorists for fire, his Detective for the firemen... and "Nothing Lasts Forever" was born.

Fox made a deal with Thorp, who expected the hardback book to become a best seller as soon as the film was officially announced. But Frank Sinatra turned down the film. And the hardback book (without the heat of the film deal) didn't become a best seller. Even with good reviews ("Single mindedly brilliant in concept and execution" - Los Angeles Times), "Nothing Lasts Forever" didn't even go to paperback until 1979.

Fifteen years later, Joel Silver was looking for a project they could make on the cheap. He had his minions search through material already owned by Fox for a script or book with a strong action story. They found "Nothing Lasts Forever" and commissioned a script.

The first person they offered the lead to was, of course, Frank Sinatra. He had played the character in the hit film "The Detective", after all. Sinatra turned it down again. Silver offered it to Robert Mitchum. Mitchum thought there was too much running and jumping for a man his age, and declined.

With the clock ticking, Silver decided to change the story from the father/estranged daughter conflict of the novel to a husband/estranged wife conflict, and hire a younger man. Steven deSouza made revisions, and turned "Nothing Lasts Forever" into "Die Hard". Bruce Willis was paid the unbelievable fee of five million dollars for his first film role... And Roderick Thorp's novel finally became a best seller!

STRUCTURE

The key to "Die Hard"s success is its adherence to the special structure of action films. The most important single element in an action script is not the protagonist, but the Villain's Plan. We can excise John McClane from "Die Hard" and we would still have a group of hostages held on the 30th floor of the Nakatomi Building by terrorist/"exceptional thief" Hans Gruber. Officer Powell might then become the protagonist. If we remove Powell from the scene, the protagonist might become FBI Agent Johnson (no, the other one). Or Holly Genero might become the protagonist, using level-headed strength to save her fellow captives. Only Hans Gruber and his plan to rob the Nakatomi Building on Christmas Eve remains the constant.

In an action script, the protagonist is reactive; it is the villain who has the active role. When Hans and his team take over the Nakatomi Building to rob its vault of 640 million dollars in negotiable bonds, they take the Christmas party crowd on the 30th floor hostage. We find out later, the hostages are an integral part of their plan. The hostages bring in the FBI, and Hans needs the FBI to shut off the power grid (which will open the vault). When Holly Genero is taken hostage, she is part of Hans' plan. One of the actions he has taken which will lead to the robbery of the Nakatomi vault.

McClane has a reactive role. His estranged wife has

been taken, and he sets out to rescue her. Before Hans took her hostage, he had no reason to rescue her. His motivation exists only because of Hans' actions. The most important character in "Die Hard" is Hans Gruber, and the character motivations for the success of the script are his. Not McClane's.

But what makes "Die Hard" into a superior script is the nexus between the Villain's Plan and the Protagonist's character arc. Though we could remove McClane from the story and still have a film, it is John McClane who turns "Die Hard" into the quintessential model for action scripts.

ORGANIC ACTION

What makes John McClane the perfect protagonist for "Die Hard" is that the external conflict forces him to confront and solve an internal conflict, leading to a single solution which solves both problems and brings peace to the protagonist.

John McClane is estranged from his wife Holly because he will not accept her as a career woman. Her career comes second to his, and his attitude is expressed in this exchange (pg 7, 8):

                    ARGYLE
          So, your lady live out here?

                    McCLANE
          The past six months.

                    ARGYLE
               (thinking about that)
          Meanwhile, you still live in New York?

                    McCLANE
          You're nosey, you know that, Argyle?

                    ARGYLE
        So, you divorced, or what?

McClane gives up.

                    McCLANE
        She had a good job, it turned into a
        great career.

                    ARGYLE
        But meant her moving here.

                    McCLANE
        Closer to Japan. You're fast.

                    ARGYLE
        So, why didn't you come?

                    McCLANE
        'Cause I'm a New York cop who used to be
        a New York kid, and I got six months backlog
        of New York scumbags I'm still trying to put
        behind bars. I don't just get up and move.

                    ARGYLE
                (to the point)
        You mean you thought she wouldn't make it
        out here and she'd come crawling on back, so
        why bother to pack?

                    McCLANE
        Like I said, Argyle.... You're fast.

McClane wants Holly to come to him both
physically (note the number of times he uses New York
in his exchange) and metaphorically (Argyle's observa-
tion that McClane would like her to come crawling back
to him). He doesn't feel the need to meet her halfway,
and we get the feeling he has flown to Los Angeles in the
hopes of taking her back to New York with him. When

they meet, McClane and Holly have this exchange (from page 16 &17).

> McCLANE
> I remember this one particular married woman,
> she went out the door so fast there was
> practically a jet wash...I mean, talk about
> your windchill factor...

> HOLLY
> Didn't we have this same conversation in
> July? Damn it, John, there was an opportu
> nity out here... I had to take it...

> McCLANE
> No matter what it did to out marriage?

> HOLLY
> My job and my title and my salary did
> nothing to our marriage except change your
> idea of what it should be.... You want to
> know my idea of a marriage? It's a partner
> ship where people help each other over the
> rough spots, console each other when there's
> a down... and when there's an up, hell, a
> little Goddamn applause or an attaboy
> wouldn't be too bad.
>> (quietly)
> I needed that, John.
>> (pause)
> I deserved that.

There's a clumsy pause as if she's challenging him
to say... something, but he sets his jaw, says
nothing.

Without being antagonistic, McClane refuses to
meet Holly halfway. He refuses to come to her. It is only
when Hans' Plan puts Holly in danger, that McClane finally realizes how much he loves her, and how uncom-

promising his stance concerning their marriage has become. Witness this exchange with Officer Powell from page 94:

> McCLANE
> Look... I'm getting a bad feeling up here...
> I'd like you to do something for me. Look up
> my wife... and tell her... tell her... I've
> been a jerk. When things panned out for her,
> I should have been behind her all the way...
> We had something great going until I screwed
> it up. She was the best thing that ever
> happened to a bum like me. She's heard me
> say I Love You a thousand times, but she
> never got to hear this... honey, I'm sorry.

It is only after he faces and conquers this internal conflict that he becomes strong enough to take on Hans (his external conflict) and rescue Holly and the other hostages. Without the external conflict from Hans' Plan, McClane would not have been forced to resolve this problem, and their marriage would have ended. The resolution for the external conflict and internal conflict intersect, creating a strong, organic plot.

THEME

The theme of "Die Hard" is probably How Far Will We Go For Love? McClane learns he would risk his life for the love of his wife, but many other characters echo this theme throughout the script.

Holly has a love of self reliance and independence so strong that she risks her life by standing up to the terrorists, as in the scene on page 54-I and 54-J where Holly confronts Hans, slyly calling him an idiot and stating that "Personally, I don't enjoy being this close to you," in order to get medical help and bathroom privileges for the other hostages.

Ellis loves to make deals, which is referred to when his character is introduced on page 12, and on page 67 where he attempts to deal with the terrorists. His love for deal making leads to his death, when the deal sours.

The terrorist Karl loves his brother Tony. When Tony is killed by McClane, Karl vows vengeance. From this point on, Karl's sole motivation is revenge against McClane for his brother's death. He is no longer an active participant in Hans' Plan, except when it intersects his own goals.

The reporter Thornburg loves breaking stories. When he first hears of the Nakatomi Tower takeover, he dumps his girlfriend to cover the story (page 53). Even after getting punched in the nose, Thornburg's response is "Did you get that?" to the camera man. Story before self.

Deputy Chief Dwayne T. Robinson loves to be officious. He would risk the lives of the hostages just for the chance of adding a little red tape to the negotiations.

Even a minor Terrorist's love for junk food takes him to the extreme of snagging a candy bar during a shoot out scene.

Hans, of course, loves material possessions. He could discuss men's fashions all day, but they are here to rob the vault of 640 million dollars. After the robbery has soured and Hans has been tossed out a broken window, what does he grab hold of? Holly's gold Rolex. He's still grabbing at possessions, even on his way down to the pavement.

VILLAIN'S SUPERIORITY

Before he reaches the pavement, Hans Gruber has shown himself to be superior in every way. Not only is his plan well thought out and ingenious, he is actually several moves ahead of everyone else. He knows the FBI will cut the power, and has planned ahead. He has a plan for every move McClane makes, from setting the fire alarms to radioing the police. His plan to open the vault at Nakatomi is complex and flawless. Hans' forethought, his "exactness and attention to every detail" has supplied a solution for every conceivable problem.

And Hans is clever enough to think on his feet. When McClane stumbles upon him on the top floor of the building, here's what happens:

```
Hans turns, looks up.
The transformation in his expression and bearing
are mind-boggling. Hands shaking, eyes filled with
fear, he swallows, looks up at McClane and in a
perfect American accent says:

                    HANS
        ...OhGodplease...don'tkill me...don't kill
        me... you're one of them, I know it...

                    McCLANE
        Whoa, easy man. I won't hurt you.
```

This scene turns into a multi-reversal. Hans talks McClane into giving him a gun. Hans then reveals his identity and aims the gun at McClane. But McClane has removed the clip, making the gun useless. But Hans has alerted Karl and Franco, who attack McClane. Which leads to the glass shooting sequence, where Hans proves his strategic superiority, and presses McClane to his point of no return which leads into the third act.

This is the first time that McClane and Hans come face to face, and it happens fairly late in the script (page 78). The relationship between hero and villain in "Die Hard" doesn't follow the "Flipside" model traditionally used in action films, where the hero and villain's similarities are accentuated.

Instead, "Die Hard" harkens back to the social consciousness films of the 1930s, like Warner Brother's "Captain Blood", where the differences between hero and villain are highlighted.

McClane and Hans are almost opposites. McClane with his working class, blue collar back ground; and Hans with his classical education and Saville Row suits. This is a battle of style and substance, with McClane's street experience pitted against what Hans read about in Time Magazine or Forbes and saw on 60 Minutes (pg 24, 68, 74). McClane and Hans' first conversation (pg 54-A) points out the contrasts between the two.

Hans' dialogue is refined, he refers to McClane as a 'party crasher'. McClane, on the other hand, makes references to game shows and cowboys, calling himself "Just the fly in the ointment, the monkey in the wrench, the pain in the ass".

One of the keys to the success of "Die Hard" is John McClane himself. He speaks in a language we can understand, rather than the stuffy, dry, pseudo intellectual and professorial language of Hans. He IS a cowboy: an individualistic man whose character is earthy and grounded in reality. A multi layered hero, who isn't afraid to admit to his fear.

In his introduction (pg 1), we see him white knuckled as the 747 lands in Los Angeles. When a fellow passenger comments on his fear of flying, McClane makes a joke about it at his own expense. He is a man who acknowledges his fears and weaknesses and has learned to live with them.

When McClane is faced with dangerous situations later on, this fear humanizes him. He is not some super human hero; but a husband, father, and very mortal man who must over come his fears to survive. He feels as we would in his situation. McClane must grow into a hero to survive. That growth is the key to a successful action script, as witnessed by "The Fugitive", "Face/Off", and "In The Line Of Fire", which follow the same pattern.

One of the most impressive aspect's of Steven de Souza's writing in "Die Hard" is the ending, where a dozen sub plots are brought to conclusion in 4 quick pages. From Hans' death, to the Nakatomi Bonds falling like Christmas snow, to Holly giving up her gold Rolex (and all the greed is symbolizes), to Argyle the limo driver's smashing the getaway car in the underground garage, to the first face-to-face meeting of hero and sidekick (McClane and Powell), to Thornburg getting punched in the nose (for being too nosey), to Dpt. Chief Robinson's officiousness being completely ignored, to Karl's last ditch revenge for his brother's death, to Sgt. Powell regaining his ability to shoot his gun, to Holly and McClane reuniting... All of this and more in the space of four flowing pages. DeSouza makes this complex web seem effortless and elegant.

By weaving together the big action story fueled by the plan of a larger than life villain, with the smaller, personal story of a husband who must find the courage to admit he is wrong before he can reconcile with his estranged wife; Steven deSouza has turned "Die Hard" into a classic action film, the model of what a genre script should strive for, and the barometer with which to measure all future action films.

Acknowledgements:

Hitchcock quotes from "Hitchcock/Trufaut", Simon & Schuster, 1967.

Shane Black quotes from lecture to SoCal Chapter of Mystery Writers Of America attended by author.

Joel Silver quotes from AP wire story.

REQUIRED READING!

Through out this book I've used a couple of Alfred Hitchcock quotes from the 1967 book "Hitchcock/ Truffaut". A few dozen words from the Master is not enough! **"Hitchcock/Truffaut" from Simon & Schuster** has over three hundred pages of valuable information straight from Hitchcock's mouth! Learn why it's important to go from biggest to smallest, flashbacks, and tons of other information. The new edition just came out, and at $20 it's a bargain. **Buy it today!** ISBN # 0-671-60429.

"Breaking Through, Selling Out, Dropping Dead" by William Bayer is another must read. Written in 1971, it is still the best common sense book on the film business. Recently reissued in paperback. ISBN # 0-87910-123-7.

William Goldman's **"Adventures In The Screen Trade"** is another must read. First published in 1982, it gives an inside view of the business as well as some great writing tips. ISBN # 0-446-51273-7.

Scr(i)pt Magazine has interviews with top screenwriters, how-to articles by professional screenwriters, market and contest info, a section listing amount-agent-company for recent script sales. The best screenwriting magazine on the market. $29.95 a year. 5638 Sweet Air Road, Baldwin, MD 21013-0007.

The Hollywood Scriptwriter is a monthly newsletter with great interviews, an annual agent's issue, and a market list. The best newsletter for new writers. $34 a year. P.O. Box 10277, Burbank, CA 91510.

The amazing **Cover Art** is by **Kevin Farrell**. Story board panel from "Double Action" a screenplay by William C. Martell.

ABOUT THE AUTHOR

William C. Martell has written seventeen produced films, including the Tom Clancy style techno-thriller "Steel Sharks" with Gary Busey, Billy Dee Williams, and Billy Warlock and two HBO World Premiere Movies: the submarine thriller "Crash Dive!" starring Frederic Forrest and Michael Dudikoff, and the sci-fi actioner "Grid Runners" starring Don "The Dragon" Wilson, Michael Dorn and Athena Massey.

His Showtime Film "Black Thunder", about a stolen stealth fighter plane, stars Michael Dudikoff and Richard Norton. Action thriller "Treacherous" stars Tia Carrere, C. Thomas Howell, and Adam Baldwin. Military thriller "The Base" was directed by Mark ("Commando", "Stephen King's Firestarter") Lester and stars Mark Decascos.

His Hitchcock-style thriller "Hard Evidence" (starring Gregory Harrison and Joan Severance) was "video pick of the week" in over two dozen newspapers, and beat the Julia Roberts film "Something To Talk About" in video rentals when both debuted the same week.

He is a columnist for Scr(i)pt Magazine, a contributor to Writer's Digest and The Hollywood Scriptwriter, and is the news editor for Dean Devlin and Roland Emmerich's Eon Magazine.

Mr. Martell was the only non-nominated screenwriter mentioned on "Siskel & Ebert's If We Picked The Winners" Oscar show in 1997.